To My Friend
Beth

COPELEY HILL

by

THEL CROSBY PERKINSON

Preface

The University of Virginia – a dream created by Thomas Jefferson himself and male bastion of well-educated "Virginia Gentlemen" -- was challenged to its very roots when married veterans of World War II arrived with their wives.

The University made a strong effort to create a tolerable environment out of the funds and means it had at its disposal.

A nearby expanse of barren hills and meadows was laid out with roads and plumbing, electricity, and sewer lines. They named it Copeley Hill - 350 dark gray trailers and 25 wooden barracks.

The Army was persuaded to part with shelter in the form of: 350 collapsible trailers and fifty long, wooden barracks. The barracks were turned into apartments for families. The collapsible trailers had the sides lifted and the entire module was enclosed with outside walls. These were for the couples. Most student-housing projects all over America had community baths. Each of our trailers was outfitted with a tiny real bathroom with tiny fixtures and a tiny hot water heater that had been designed for the Army trailers. We were blessed not having to go to the bathroom down the road, or shower with fifteen other people.

In the winter the trailers were cold; in the summer they were hot. But they were ours.

On the other hand, Copeley was nothing but gray. Dark gray. The Navy had generously donated hundreds of gallons of paint for Copeley. It was a gray that was so ominous and ugly it made one's heart sink. The truth was the color had been developed to camouflage the battleships to blend with the ocean!

The real story of Copeley Hill lay in the unique lives being lived in each trailer. No two were alike. Personalities, background, choices, dreams changed as one moved past #77, to #76, then across to #65. It was a kaleidoscope of stories being lived and created, day by day, entirely inhabited by young people nineteen to thirty-five.

With all husbands in college and a consistent, severe lack of money and outside stimulation, this small universe spun on a tilted axis. Sacrifice by the wives was a daily expectation. It radiated out from the support system for the student-husbands like a beacon.

Work was a blessing because it got the women out of the vapid atmosphere of relentless quiet when husbands were home studying. there was an unspoken given that we would all do our best; we would be stalwart; we would be patient; we would try to enjoy. In essence, we would be the young women who set the stage to become the "June Cleavors" of the fifties and sixties.

There were three "institutions" on the hill: the Community House, the Wash House and the Copeley Hill Market.

The Community House held the office and meeting rooms. It was an old Victorian House. No heat but kerosene stoves.

The Wash House housed ten washing machines and ten huge sinks. The residents signed up for 1 ½ hours maximum; and by the time clothes were washed, run through ringers, rinsed twice by hand and placed in a big basket – WET – to be taken home by strong husbands, we were over that routine. But not quite...they had to be hung on lines between the trailers.

That place was a cesspool of gossip and news and was great fun in between the shouting over the washing machines, repeating wild gossip and telling hysterical jokes. Faces you hadn't seen for weeks you'd bump into there. Friends were made and enemies were formed in the Wash House. Clothes got cleaned and life went on.

The Copeley Hill Market was a one-of-a-kind grocery store in an Army issued Quonset hut. It was an arched building made of corrugated steel. No insulation, no precise lighting, no nothing. Slightly tired vegetables and two cold boxes: one for meat, one for milk and cheese and beer, and soft drinks. White bread, only.

But it was a blessing! It was the only grocery store for miles and they gave us credit when we needed it. The name of the owner eludes my mind and generosity of heart has never left my memory.

There is little to tell about Copeley – several paragraphs, that is all. There is much to tell about the couples. Together, the stories show the belief in the rainbow and the character it took to follow a difficult trail to achieve the pot of gold for themselves and this country.

Unfortunately, the dark demanding side of the journey wore heavily on the marriages and began to pull them apart. Then, destroy them. Within ten years, the divorce rates for this segment of the American population reach a staggering 67%; the highest the country had ever seen.

We didn't fail. But our marriages did.

Forward

This is about the bright, lovely generation of Americans born in the 1920's.

World War I had been over for several years and the country was ready for a joyful, lighthearted era of "Oh, you kid!" "Twenty-three scadoo!", or maybe "Life is just a bowl of cherries!". It was the era women bobbed their hair for the first time, and rolled their stockings to their knees, just below their short skirts, and became flappers. They got the right to vote and they smoked cigarettes in long holders.

Some didn't. My mother did.

The men began to dress more dashingly, a la Scott Fitzgerald, in wide slacks, v-necks sweaters, raccoon coats and their hair slicked back.

The black Bottom or the Charleston dance craze swept the land. The blues and ragtime of New Orleans and Memphis were right behind. And overlaying it all was the lush elegance of George Gershwin's new American music that began to outline what this young generation's tastes would be.

Then, in 1927, the stock market crashed and took our country and our families down into the horrifying Great Depression. During our pre-teen years, the 30's, we were frightened children watching our families desperately struggling through a time that threatened to engulf us all in poverty and starvation.

There was no one to save us but ourselves. There were soup lines everywhere--everyday. We didn't complain often. How could you complain to a neighbor who had lost everything?

But always, there were the movies. Fred Astaire and Ginger Rogers dancing to the music of Gershwin and Cole Porter showed America – especially young America – how to be elegant and romantic, they gave us back our dreams.

When President Roosevelt was elected, he developed brilliant government strategies to turn the country around, so that by the time the 1940's arrived, our country was slowly becoming a much happier place and some things were still right with our world: our doors could be left unlocked, one's word was not to be broken, and the truth was always told (most of the time).

Men did not swear in front of ladies; girls did not have illegitimate babies; and families did not have two cars.

In 1938, "no" was "no", no matter what. We had urges and surges but they were always kept under control. The fear of God and our parents might have helped that a bit! We smooched in the park, we flirted, and we sang along with Ella Fitzgerald and Frank Sinatra and danced ourselves into oblivion to Tommy Dorsey. We did our schoolwork, we obeyed our parents; and we talked incessantly on the phone (often on a phone-line that was shared with another customer called a "party line").

My generation jitterbugged and Lindy Hopped through years that were uncertain; and we be-bopped in our bobby socks and saddle shoes into young adulthood. The music and the dancing filled our young lives, and made up for a lack of money and a deep sadness in America.

Then came the war.

The Japanese, who stood outside our gates daring us to come out and fight, were convinced that the "drugstore cowboys" would fall apart within six months and the war would be over.

However, not every young American male made it into battle. One out of every nine recruits was rejected because they had malnutrition as children, they became malnourished because of the depression: no food, no money – statistics showed that if one member of a family was half-starved, the entire family was half-starved. So, within the United States of America in the 30's, one family out of nine – maybe more – had malnutrition.

Fortunately, the rest of the young men accepted for the military were strong and healthy. What came roaring into battle were some of the greatest warriors in history. Not only could Americans fight, but they were brilliant in battle strategies. They also were incredibly brave and feisty!

Above all, Americans had integrity. While the pattern of the Japanese was to rape, kill and plunder, Americans never did. There Germans tortured and killed prisoners and civilians. Americans never did. All the wholesome collective consciousness of the American nation love of country, pinup girls, and Mom's apple pies were taken into battle by American soldiers (twenty-one years after their fathers had fought in World War I), and made them unbeatable!

In 1944 Congress moved to create a bill – the G.I. Bill – that would help the returning soldiers buy homes with no down payment, insurance policies of all types at cost, free medical care and a fully paid education at a college or training school including books, tuition and $70.00 a month for living expenses.

However, the opposition to such "madness" was strong and vocal.

"It will bankrupt the country."

"It will create loafers and deadbeats."

"The married soldiers will make terrible students! You cannot be a father and be a student. This has NEVER been permitted."

They forgot that G.I.'s grew up fast in foxholes and during bombing raids.

The powerful American Legion puts its weight behind the G.I. Bill and pushed it to the forefront; it never wavered from that position throughout ridiculous maneuverings by the Senate and House. This was a political hot potato that seethed back and forth, bitterly for months. Finally, a committee of seven Senators and seven Representatives was put together for the purpose of working out a compromise bill.

Surprisingly, within a matter of days, all seven Senators and three of the Representatives agreed to pass the Bill. However, a parsimonious old politician, Rep. John Rankin o Mississippi led three others against it. In the meantime, one vote was still out on the

Representative side. The deciding vote belonged to John Gibson of Georgia. Since he had been called home on an emergency, Gibson left a proxy vote with Rankin saying "compromise". Incredibly, Rep. John Rankin refused to honor the proxy, thereby sealing the fate of the G.I. Bill, which would automatically die by 10 a.m. the following morning.

The American Legion went into action against Rankin's arrogance enlisting the aid of radio stations throughout the state to broadcast appeals for information as to Gibson's whereabouts; and operators called his home continually until he finally responded around 11 p.m.

State police drove him to Waycross, Georgia. A waiting military car drove him to Jacksonville, Florida. When he was driven to the Jacksonville airport, a plane, sent by the American Legion was revved up waiting to fly him to Washington!

Representative John Gibson of Douglas, Georgia arrived in Washington, D.C. about 7 a.m. and cast his deciding vote three hours later. Because of the American Legion one of the great pieces of American legislature as passed: THE G.I. BILL

And so this generation of young Americans born in the 20's took their unbelievable opportunity, took their hard work, their strengths and their dreams and together pushed this country into an era of growth and prosperity and education never seen before in the history of the world. Seven million of them!

It is said history will record this generation as "The Late, Great American Generation". We accept that accolade…we were so beautiful in so many ways.

We still are.

Copeley Hill, 1948

We were twenty-one when we got married. It was 1948. The war was over, and my husband was a law student at the University of Virginia.

"If it was good enough for Ambassador Kennedy's son, and President Roosevelt's son, it's good enough for us," we'd say to each other. "We'll manage it somehow." Sheer bravado! Our income was $150.00 -- 75.00 from government and $75.00 from my studio -- per month.

We lived on Copley Hill, the married student's trailer complex, along with three hundred and fifty-nine other married couples. We lived in three hundred and sixty dark, gray, small, identical trailers. Each had a dark green front door. Altogether, the effect was hideous.

The sight often created a sinking feeling in me. When the feeling persisted, I did something about it. I painted my door red -- bright red.

It was the perfect break in a rhythm of gray. I adored my door, and admired it and congratulated myself again and again.

My euphoria died quickly when the student mayor of Copeley Hill came to call.

"Perk," Mac spoke to my husband. "We are happy to have you both as neighbors and I've come to welcome you. However, we are not happy about that red door."

"What's the door doing to make you unhappy?" Perk asked. He was an innocent.

"It isn't in keeping with the Hill. Did anyone give you permission?" He was unmistakably annoyed.

"Noooo." I give Perk credit. He was unflappable. "And I'm almost positive there's nothing in the lease."

Mac stood up. "I've called a special council meeting for tomorrow night to handle some extra business and I would appreciate your cooperation when we discuss this further."

"I'll come," I interrupted. "Perk has a law meeting, but I'm free." The mayor appeared not to hear me.

"Uh, excuse me, Mac…"

He turned in the doorway, "We only deal with students, not their wives. That's the way it goes here."

I wish I'd known the word "macho," then but it was an unknown in those days. And God forbid if a "nice girl" said "damn" or "go suck an orange".

The mayor's attitude was clear. The men knew best, and women must not make waves. The men would make the decision about my door, which meant it would go.

I made a decision too. My door would remain red. This was my home, — my feeding ground, my dappled space under the trees, my place to drop cubs. This was female territory and so was the damn door, go suck an orange!

Then I cried.

My new husband was beside himself.

I threatened.

My new husband told the mayor he had a problem.

I said no.

My new husband said no to the mayor.

The mayor complained to the President of the College and an appointment was set up for all parties to meet.

Good morning, gentlemen," said the President. "You have a problem, I hear. Suppose we have a seat and quietly discuss this."

"Yes, sir," said the mayor. "Perk and his wife have painted their trailer door red against the wishes of the Council. We need to discuss this matter."

Perk sat there, a little sunk by the entire episode.

"She painted the door red?" This to Perk.

"Well, yes, she did, sir. She says unless the lease says we can't do it, she'll just keep painting it; and she says the 'Hill' is ugly and needs some color."

The President smiled. "She's right, you know. And Mr. Mayor, DOES the lease say you can't paint the door?"

"No, sir, but it does say you can't paint the trailer."

"But they can paint inside?"

"Oh, sure, ...but not...'

Here the President interrupted. "Mr. Mayor, I'm all for it – this door thing. How long have we had Copeley Hill? Four years?"

"Three, sir."

"And not one soul ever painted a door?"

"I don't think so, sir."

"Well, I'm glad the little lady did." He leveled a serious look at both students. "Has it occurred to you gentlemen that these young wives are living an unusual life here? It's got to be tough on them. So if a wife wants a red door, why can't she have a red door? Anything else?" The President stood up.

"No, sir, that was all." Perk said. "I would like to thank you for Thelma. Sorry we took your time, Mr. Darden."

"That's alright, Mr. Perkinson, this was a lot different from most of my problems." He smiled.

That was the first week of January. By the first week of March, most of the doors were painted – purple, yellow, blue, orange and one red door.

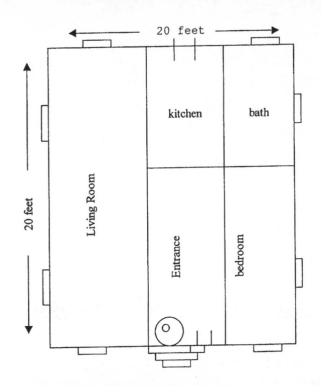

20 feet

20 feet

Living Room

kitchen

bath

Entrance

bedroom

**Copeley Hill
Army
Trailer
20' x 20'**

Thel

Trailer Living Room
Thel, Mo', Hawk, Parlier

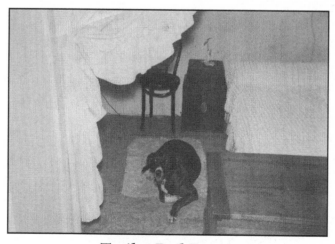

Trailer Bed Room
School Mascot

The Mighty Mo

We moved into our trailer on Copeley Hill on a Saturday. This was Mo's cleaning day.

I looked out my window and saw a tiny person in a man's flight suit – her husband's – with the sleeves and legs rolled up like huge doughnuts around her wrists and ankles.

A mop was propped against the trailer steps. Mo sat next to it with a bottle of wine beside her. She looked a bit like Dopey, one of the Seven Dwarfs, as she sat there slowly sipping wine.

She also looked interesting.

I went out to introduce myself. "I'm Thel Perkinson," I said.

"Marge Osana," she replied. "They call me 'Mo'." The voice was a little world weary, the tone superior, but it was softened by a southern accent. She took a long draw on her cigarette and a long look at me. Frankly, I don't think I passed muster, but she chatted a few minutes longer, ground her cigarette into the grass and announced, "this is my cleaning day, I've got to go." At that, she disappeared into the trailer with the wine.

During the week, I rarely saw Mo. She worked long hours in the Medical Records Section of the University Hospital and entered her trailer exhausted at night.

Rick, her deadly attractive husband of temperamental Cuban descent, studied each night at the Engineering School. Mo was always alone. Sometimes they ate together, but then he'd leave and she'd clean the dishes and fall into bed.

Each Saturday Mo emerged in her flight suit to shake a rug or shake a mop. When her trailer was done, she'd plop on the steps in the sun to smoke her cigarette and sip her wine.

As she cleaned, she flung the doors and windows of her trailer wide-open, classical music spilling full blast out of that ugly little trailer. What a ritual!

14

Gradually we put our friendship together. And as we sat there on the steps drinking wine, our stories began to emerge.

I told her about the great love of my life, my grand passion. Not my husband, Perk, but an earlier love whose name was George Hopkins. He was the most wonderful man, urbane, fun loving, fine. . .and handsome beyond belief.

"He was an older man – ten years older than me. He was a Captain in the blue Devil Army Corps in Italy."

I had met him when he was recuperating from a grenade-shattered elbow in the Army Hospital. After he was transferred, we called and visited and I fell in love.

I sighed. "I loved him. I'll always love him...but it didn't turn out."

"What happened to him?"

I looked at her and realized tears were stinging my eyes. "He married his home town sweetheart."

"And you?"

"I went to New York to study drama. That didn't work out either. I worked too hard, studied too hard, didn't eat right. I had to come home because I got sick."

"And probably had a broken heart." Mo said, nodding her head wisely. "Hearts can do that...absolutely...no question."

"Umm." I mused. "I know I got awfully sick. I'd be talking or laughing or eating one minute, and tears would be spilling the next."

"Did you go back to New York?" she asked.

"No. I went back to college at home. I majored in music. That's where I met Perk."

By then Mo had finished her trailer and we had both finished her wine and were mellowing out in the sunshine.

"I tell you, Puss," she said affectionately, "You're still an innocent." She paused, "How many men have you been with?"

"Ye gods, what a question!" I thought. "No one asks questions like that!"

"Never mind...never mind...she said impatiently, "I can tell from your prissy expression you wouldn't tell the truth anyway." Then she let out a whoop. "Tell you one thing, Thel honey, grand passions don't just sit there doing nothing. Grand passions sweep you off your feet into wonderful arms and moments to die for!"

She leveled her gaze at me. "You're lucky," she said, blowing smoke. "I figure most of the human race never even knows one grand passion. Trust me."

She dragged on her cigarette. "Just look at me," she said, "I've been married three times and ..."

"Three times? Rick is your third husband?" I was thunderstruck.

How could this plain, slightly built woman who never wore makeup have been married three times? She wore braids so tight they pulled her eyebrows up half an inch. She couldn't have been married three times! I was looking at a femme fatale!

"My god." I said. "How old are you Mo? How old were you when you got married the first time?"

"Sixteen, the first time," she giggled, "and thirty now."

"How old is Rick? He's not thirty, is he?"

"Nooo, he's twenty-three."

"And you? Have you had a grand passion?" Somehow I knew the answer.

She looked at me, narrowing her eyes, slowly exhaling smoke, before she said, "You can bet on it."

I was impressed. "Some woman," I thought. "No wonder she's so smart!"

And she was. She was also a little cynical — a lot cynical actually — with a sharp, biting wit, a brilliant mind, and a reared-in-Southern-private-schools attitude.

The trouble with the 'brilliant mind' part was her conviction that hers was the only brilliance around.

Still, I learned to love her and not hold it against her – that I was twenty-one and naïve, and she had LIVED. Way down deep, I knew I was smart too.

Mo wore leather brogues with the rubber soles. Her feet were small but because she carried enormous medical files up and down ladders all day at the hospital, the sponge rubber soles had splayed out around the entire shoe. They were HUGE.

"Hey Mo," Pres Luck yelled from his trailer one day, "don't forget, when you get rid of those shoes I want 'em. I'll dip 'em in bronze and use 'em for door stops." It became a running joke.

"Smart ass," Mo would mutter around the cigarette she held tight in her mouth. As always, the men laughed boisterously. And Mo would laugh too.

Other times she didn't laugh at all.

The fact was: Mo couldn't buy any shoes. Rick handled the money, and he said they couldn't afford it. Mo earned the money, but she couldn't have shoes. Still, she loved him a lot.

Like Mo, I put my earnings in Perk's name. That was the norm on Copeley Hill. I hated it. The way I spent it wasn't to his liking either, but that, too, was the norm on Copeley Hill. The truth was this endeavor of marriage and college was harder on the wives than on the husbands. I was amazed to learn the great majority of wives had been to college – while the great majority of husbands had not.

The year before Rick's graduation, Mo decided to buy him a Jeep, a new one.

"He'll kill you," I said. "You can't spend money that way. Are you totally nuts?"

"Now, Puss, I've got it all figured out. The dealer is going to let me make payments for a year until he's got the down payments plus two months. So, next year I'll give him the Jeep. God, he'll faint!"

"Unh, unh, girl. Where's the money coming from?"

Stuff like this could tear a marriage apart on Copeley Hill. We were there for the husbands, not them for us.

"I'm going to save my lunch money – and -- she was clearly resolved, "my wine money and..."

"Nope." I stated flatly. "Not the wine money. Oh, what the heck; I'll buy the wine from now on and we'll keep it at your house." By now I'd grown to really like our Saturday sipping and saying sessions on the steps.

As the months passed, Mo got downright frail. Her thick braids and her shoes were the biggest things about her.

"You look like a sparrow." I said. "You can't work like a horse and not eat." She was too thin and too pale. "Can't you take a sandwich?"

She looked at me. "Sometimes, yes; most times no. No food to spare."

I heard that statement on the Hill more times than I care to remember. Once the money was gone, it was gone until payday. Some parents helped. Some didn't. It was hard.

Couples were truly poor: no movies, no car, no clothes. And television hadn't been invented yet, so we only had the radio, which couldn't be played, because husbands were studying.

The comfort of ample food was sporadic. Still, we persevered.

A year passed, and Rick's graduation drew near. To celebrate, a group of us had ordered a keg of beer. The wives fixed food, and we decorated the new Jeep standing at the curb with streamers.

A classmate dropped Rick off. He stopped dead in his tracks, dumbfounded.

18

"God," he said, "whose is THAT?"

"Yours," we yelled, whooping and laughing.

His eyes bugged, "Mine?" H turned to Mo. "What are they talking about?"

"I bought you a Jeep." Mo said. "I wanted to give you something wonderful."

"Where'd you get the money?" he gasped.

"I did without lunches and wine and paid by the week." She said proudly. "I wanted to show you how much I love you...to show you I'm proud of you."

We stood listening, realizing this was, indeed, a rather wonderful moment.

Mo looked at Rick with a side-glance. "Now you can teach me how to drive, Rick!" she said teasingly.

We turned to watch Rick. His mouth tightened and his face reddened. He slowly shook his head. "I dunno, Mo. You know how emotional you are. I'd be afraid you'd wreck it."

The silence that followed was unbearable. We stood frozen for a split second, then we headed for our trailers, en masse, to "get the food." After a while, we reappeared.

All was calm between them and it would have been a shame to waste the beer, the food and the Jeep rides. So we partied half the night with our blankets spread between the trailers on the grass – the way we always did on Copeley Hill.

The next day was Saturday; however, it became obvious to all of us that a new agenda had been decreed at Rick and Mo's. There was no flight suit, no cleaning, no Mo.

"She's gone to town," Rick said.

"Where?" we asked.

"Nobody's damn business. Her exact words."

As the day progressed, I decided to have a sip or two of wine, sit on the steps and wait for my friend. I felt nervous about her.

The Copeley Hill bus came up the hill. Off stepped Margaret Ann Brisbane Fortescue Taylor Osana, in heels and new dress. She clutched shopping bags, large and small, about her. The closer she came, the prettier she got. Glory of glories, this caterpillar had cut her hair, put on make-up (a lot of it) and become a butterfly!

I began shrieking at the top of my voice – Incredible! Omigod, incredible!" People poured out of the trailers.

Rick opened the door, Perk dashed around the side of the trailer, Pres and Mickey stumbled out yelling, "What…what?"

"Look." I gasped and pointed up the hill toward Mo.

"Jesus," Pres breathed, "look at her! She's gorgeous!"

"Tell me that isn't a sight." Marge boozer crowed.

But Rick thought otherwise. "What the hell has she done to herself?" Rick growled under his breath.

"I don't know, but she's really beautiful." I glanced at Rick. "Rick, don't blow this," I implored. "She's a wonderful girl," my voice trailed off. By then, more and more people were gathering and yelling and clapping.

The next few moments are a bit fuzzy, but in the melee I clearly remember Mo telling Rick to shut his "mean mouth" and to "just wait'll you get the bills. Then you'll really something to yell about!"

Mo stormed into her trailer with all of us still whistling and yelling our approval. Then she stormed back out and roared at Rick, "And no more flight suit. Ever!"

All afternoon I looked out the window for signs of Mo. And just as the sun set, I saw her sitting there, on her trailer steps, wearing a new cotton dress, smoking and sipping. She ran her fingers through her curly, short hair as the long rays warmed her.

"Hi, Puss," she grinned, looking up at my window. "Come on over, and bring a glass."

The Piano Studio

I stood looking at the printing on the door of my new studio in Charlottesville. It said: Don Warner Studio of Popular Music. "In-cred-i-ble," I said out loud. "Incredible!"

My mind slipped back to that crisp fall day, a year ago, when Don Warner asked me: "How would you like to open a studio for me in Charlottesville when you and Perk move there?" This was the man who owned The Don Warner School of Popular Music in Richmond, Virginia.

I had learned his chord method in one year when I was a senior in high school (I had studied seven years of classical music before that, beginning when I was five). Then, I'd gone to college in New York, and now I was teaching for him in Richmond.

And now here he was, making me this astounding offer.

"Well," I said, "I'd really like it, but Perk and I won't have any money to do that."

"You don't have to. I'll set you up."

"You'll set me up?" I repeated his words, slowly. "How come?"

"I've been wanting to expand the business."

"Un-hunh."

"If the right person came along to run a new studio.'"

"Un-hunh."

"...and you're going to Charlottesville and it's a natural!" Don's voice was positive.

"Don, I don't know if I'm capable..." My voice trailed. "I don't know anything about business."

"You know the method, don't you?"

"Yes…"

"You need a job, don't you?"

"Yes, sir."

"Well, you've got a job! And you'll have plenty of help from us. We'll find the studio and the furniture, and we'll do the advertising and cut the money 50 – 50."

"And I can teach the method plus anything I want to add?"

"You're already doing that", he laughed. "I hear you in your studio teaching scales in jazz rhythms and carrying on about the proper touch and proper pedal."

"I don't exactly carry on," I grinned.

"No…you don't. You're really a marvelous teacher. You are but you're fun. The students love you!"

"Thanks," I said. "I really want them to play well. I try very hard."

"And that's why you've got a studio of your own, if you want it." I did.

Months later, I was standing in my new studio when someone asked "This your studio?"

I slowly turned around to see a very attractive person was standing in the open door.

"All mine," I said proudly.

"I'm Jerry Ann Keane," she smiled chipperly.

In that instant, I knew I had my first friend in Charlottesville, maybe even a lifelong friend, but she died four years later.

Sadly, she got polio while she was pregnant – remember? There was no Jonas Salk, no polio shots in those days. They put her in an iron lung to help her and keep her alive until the baby came.

Dr. Nokes, a most wonderful obstetrician at the University hospital, slept in a hospital bed that had been wheeled in and placed beside the iron lung. He slept there five nights out of seven and sometimes seven, if things were not going well…he was that determined to save her. But he couldn't.

By some miracle he managed to save the baby. A girl – Jerry Ann Keane Korally. Almost as cute as her mother. At first, the Keane family took the baby to help Chuck, who was totally bereft. Then they decided they wanted to keep her, unfortunately. There was court battle, but Chuck won and raised Jerry Ann himself.

But that winter morning, standing there with my new friend, I viewed the world as golden and safe. I had a new husband, a new life and a new music studio. My future stretched out in front of me enchantingly, and I couldn't wait to live it!

My mind was pierced into focus by the sharp ringing of the phone. When I answered, I heard a lovely voice inquiring about lessons.

"I'm Mrs. Lentz and I've always wanted to play popular piano."

"Have you had music training or are you a beginner?"

"I've had music training," she answered.

"That's good! That way you'll be playing really well by Christmas."

"How much do you charge?" The lovely voice continued.

"Two dollars for thirty minutes," I replied.

"When can I come," she asked. "Tomorrow?"

"No-o-o, I'm booked tomorrow. How's the next day? At 10 a.m.?"

"Perfect!" She was clearly excited. "I'll be there."

My first pupil! And my second friend.

I've never forgotten that marvelous Muzzy Lentz! She was beautiful and she was married to an important professor, Dr. Lentz. They had three children my age and lived a rather glamorous life holding court from a three- story home on the prestigious Loop. Mr.

Jefferson designed this connected row of homes on campus for the top professors and their families when he designed the University of Virginia. Thus, the architecture flowed beautifully throughout the grounds and created a romantic, elegant atmosphere that time had never changed.

I turned back to Jerry Ann, "Now, where were we?" I smiled.

Jerry Ann paused, "I was just getting ready to ask you how does one become the director of a jazz studio?"

"Have you got all day!" I grinned.

"No, but I've got a couple of hours tomorrow. I'll take you for a long lunch." She paused, "Let's see if you make it into a feature interview for the station. I'll bill 'em for lunch!"

"Publicity!" I thought, "What a break!" I happily agreed to the meeting.

The next day Jerry Ann picked me up at the studio, and we settled ourselves in a sunny window of a nearby restaurant.

"So," I said. "Tell me what you do at the station, I mean."

"I'm a copywriter and I do live interviews, too. It's a wonderful job. I love my boss. Guess who he is! He was vice admiral under Admiral Halsey, who defeated the Japanese Navy – Tom Corruthers!"

"Tell me some more..."

"Well..." she got a mischievous look on her face. "I went to Sweet Briar College — don't hold that against me. My folks live in Farmington and belong to the country club. Don't hold that against me either, and I'm engaged to a poor, but proud, photographer, Chuck Korally. You'll like him!" She laughed out loud.

"You know what? You're pretty funny!" I said delightedly.

"You're pretty funny, too. Are you smart?"

"Yep."

"I already knew that," she said. "Now, let's begin," and she took out a note pad.

"So, Miz Piano Teacher, how'd you learn jazz?"

I looked at her, surprised. "I expected you to ask me about my studio and maybe life on Copeley Hill." I shook my head, slowly. How...did...I...learn...jazz," I mused out loud.

Terry interrupted, "Here's what I want you to do. Just tell it. I'll do the editing later."

"I guess I got it from Tinny," I said musingly. "Tinny was my nurse when I was a baby. She'd scoop me up and dance with me as she hummed a funny *ztt, zzztt* through her teeth. She'd cake walk or Charleston or 'slum it,' and I could feel the music and the movement through her body."

"Tinny! What a marvelous name!" Jerry interrupted. "Tell me more."

"Well, Tinny taught me to sway to the blues and strut to ragtime. Actually, Tinny taught me all the songs and all the steps. I guess she taught me part of who I am. I was Tinny's 'jazz baby'."

"How old were you?" asked Jerry.

"Oh, six, seven months. She'd dance with me in her arms; and then when I could walk, she began to teach me to dance in step with her."

I paused to consider the influences. "But you have to realize I was born in the Roaring Twenties...the Jazz Age. Would you believe my mother was a flapper?" Her black hair was bobbed, and her stockings were rolled to the knees. She was adorable in those short dresses. Daddy called her 'Fifi Dorsey'! "She and my father would put on the Victrola and dance and dance in our living room maybe to Gershwin or sometimes George M. Cohen. They were so beautiful like something out of F. Scott Fitzgerald." My voice wandered off.

26

"My word, what memories! What would you do?"

"I'd make them pick me up and dance with me, too!" I laughed.

"You know," said Jerry, "I'm, what? Three years younger than you? I barely remember any of this, not the music or the clothes or anything."

"Dear Lord," I said, "and I remember everything: the music, the clothes, the hair, the dances, even the furniture! I remember the Sunday dinners, the dresses Mamma smocked for me. This is amazing! I didn't realize!" I exclaimed.

"And this is going to be a good interview." Jerry said quietly. Now, tell about learning to play."

"Over a period of time my attention moved from dancing to the piano, and I became obsessed with all those notes being pushed down by my mother and by the sales ladies in the music section in the basement of the five-and-tens. Lordy, could those women play jazz!"

"Did your mother play a lot?! Jerry asked.

"Sundays. It was the Sundays that were so wonderful." My memories were taking on a life of their own. "We always had company. The table groaned with wonderful foods and desserts and homemade wine and cigars and Mamma played and everybody sang from Mamma's pile of sheet music."

I paused for a minute thoughtfully. "To this day, when I smell cigar smoke I think of my courtly father solemnly placing paper cigar rings on my fingers and blowing smoke circles. All the men smoked cigars after Sunday dinner and they engaged in quiet serious conversations. It gave me such a fine, strong sense of men."

Jerry Ann interrupted. "You know, I'm struck by two facts: one, that I am from this same era, so are my friends; and two, no one speaks of that time the way you do." She pondered for a minute. "How come?"

My eyes widened, "You don't remember ragtime tunes or the different dances or the flappers? Wasn't your mom a flapper?"

"Nope," Jerry said, "I don't. I just remember a childhood memory here and there. You remember everything!"

"Everything." I nodded vigorously. "And I remember, at three, telling my mother to put me up to the piano, show me the first note of a certain piece of sheet music and go away. By the time I had picked out a melody and had it memorized, my legs invariably went numb. The ritual was: I would scream bloody murder, Mamma would come running and lift me off the stool, and set me in a chair because I couldn't stand! 'My legs are dead, I'd insist.

"What a funny story...what a character you were! So ...what happened then?"

"You want more?"

"A lot ," she answered. "I've got a beginning, now I need a middle and an end..."

"Okay." I took a deep breath. "But let's order some tea. I need it!"

The hot tea was a lovely comfort and it gave me a chance to catch my breath and to decide how to tell the rest of the story.

"Here's the middle," I said. "I got so I could play every tune with one finger, and on Sunday I insisted Mamma put some music up. She'd play the bass and I'd play the melody.

"When I turned six, things changed drastically. Up until then, I was 'amazing', a 'wonderful little jazz musician'. I should have 'been on the stage.' But at six, the general consensus was that I should seriously study piano. They hired a beautiful young teacher who came each week to teach me. Ruth Dau tell, and she was wonderful, but she was classical.

I asked Jerry. "Guess what the first thing she said was?"

"What?"

" 'No more jazz. No more playing by ear. You must learn to read notes, honey'."

28

"WHAT?"

"That was it. Suddenly, jazz wasn't okay. It was the early 30's, America had been through the crash and was deep into the depression. It was moving from the flappers and vo-dee-oh-do and moving toward an ultraconservative, cautious mindset. 'Ladies did not play jazz.'"

"What did you do?" Jerry asked, leaning across her teacup.

"I played classical, that's what I did."

"Ye Gods, how long did this go on?" jerry asked

"For nine years. I turned out to be a 'gifted child' and everyone felt I must aim for the Walter Demrosch School – you know, Juilliard – and a concert career."

"Is that what you wanted?"

"Nobody asked me," I replied. "Anyway, where else would I go? There was no place – no music school – where I could study jazz."

"So?"

"So suddenly my father was transferred to Richmond, Virginia and I got a new teacher: Lucy Lake. She charged sixteen dollars a month – a fortune- and she was to prepare me for the New York auditions. To make matters worse, Lucy was this genteel lady with an imposing bosom who always wore a large hat as she taught the Leschetizy method. She spoke with a broad A. She was brilliant, but humorless," I paused. "I can still hear her saying, 'control, control… you MUST control the instrument'."

"And the ending?" Jerry queried.

"I quit. It was too much for a jazz baby! Three years with Lucy was all I could manage."

Jerry leaned forward, "And then what?"

"I told everyone I'd never play again. That I had practiced two and three hours a day for years and no one wanted to hear me…that I couldn't play popular music at parties…that…that I quit!"

"Boy," breathed Jerry, "did they have a fit?"

"Whew, more than a fit!" I replied ruefully. "But I kept saying I wanted to study popular piano. I wanted to study the chord method at the Don Warner Studios. And that's what I did. My parents viewed it as a phase. Because I was such a trained musician, Don decided that if he could bring the ear alive again, I just might play some really fine jazz." I sighed and leaned back in my chair.

"Hold it," Jerry suddenly said. "I gotta to the restroom. Order some more tea and a dessert…any dessert, I don't care," and hurried off.

As Jerry settled herself back at the table, "Now don't quit, don't let down, keep the story going. How'd you get the studio?" She asked, leading me into the ending.

"I learned to teach because Don insisted. He gave me three young pupils to teach at his studios on Saturday, when I wasn't in classes at school."

"How'd you do?"

"Pretty good," I stated "*Very* good, really. And I had those kids playing like mad within four or five months and, get this, with beautiful hand position – like Ruth Dantell taught me – by putting a quarter or dimes on the back of each hand while they were doing scales. If it didn't fall off, the money was theirs to keep!"

Jerry whooped, "That's the damnest thing!"

I grinned. "I know, I know, and I had'em doing those scales in jazz rhythms."

Jerry interrupted, "Jazz scales?"

"Yep," I replied, "but here's the finishing touch." I grinned wryly, "I found myself talking 'Lucy talk'. 'Control the instrument, control the instrument'!

Naturally, I drew a complete blank from my students." I broke into laughter.

"Well, you'd sure draw a blank from me," Jerry assured me, "and I've four years of music."

"Unh-unh," I shook my head, "not if I turned the piano bench the long way, sat you down in front of me straddling the bench, made you put your hands on mine and I played the music so you could feel the control of the instrument."

"No, no, no!" Jerry erupted with a burst of laughter. "That's too funny!"

Yes," I nodded emphatically. I was grinning from ear to ear. "Pretty hot stuff, huh?"

"How'd it work?" She asked.

"I rewired their nerve endings," I hooted. "Six months…six months, and they were astonishing the way they began to get the feel, the touch, the attitude of jazz!"

Jerry looked at me quietly for a long moment. Her eyes narrowed slightly as she searched for something, for the connection.

"Just like Tinny," she stated emphatically.

"Yes," I nodded. "Just like Tinny – and Mamma – and Ruth – and Lucy – and Don."

"And Thelma," Jerry added.

SKIP AND JENNY

Skip Crockett was short and funny. Jenny was blond, sweet and a country girl from Luray, Virginia.

Skip had been a sailor on the Indianapolis aircraft carrier. Jenny worked as a hairdresser to help Skip through school.

They lived four trailers up – right next door to Anne and Bill Dingledine – and they were great neighbors because they were always good company.

Sometimes, Jenny would repeat the advice her big- mouthed, busy-bodied customers who said things like: "Now, Jenny, you're going to have to hold yourself up and learn the social rules. You are going to be married to an attorney, and you'll need to dress well. You'll need to know all of the rules of social etiquette, and, dear, you must be well read."

At times they shattered her days. After work she'd fret about her ability to be the person they said she should be. If I were there, I'd say "Hon, they can't hold a candle to you. You're smart in business. Skip obviously loves you. You're a good wife, and, besides, you make the best chicken gravy in the South!"

Almost always, she would smile.

Skip was a country boy and smart. He wasn't private- school, intellectual-family smart, but he was common sense smart. Even in law school, this was an asset.

Unfortunately, Skip also had a chronic case of diarrhea that could create a stir in a lecture class at the law school when he'd suddenly scramble for the door. Fortunately, he had sense enough to quietly explain the situation to his professors, who took race for the restroom in their strides.

Our crowd was partying together one snowy Saturday night. We pooled food and drink – and shared our triumphs and our worries and as the whiteness grew on the landscape outside, our intimacy grew in the cozy warmth inside.

The boys began to talk of the war. For some reason Skip, whose own happy glow usually shone forth, began to take over the conversation. That night he led us on a dark and gruesome journey into the watery hell that was his life on the Indianapolis.

The ship was torpedoed and sunk by the Japanese. 1,400 survivors found themselves afloat, a mass of human seaweed in the middle of the Pacific Ocean. That night, the sharks found them and began to circle.

One by one, the men were attacked, screaming as an arm or leg would be bitten off and the water around them turned red with blood. Sometimes five or six screamed at the same time. At others, more. The voices would suddenly still as the sharks pulled them under for the kill.

Skip floated amid blood and screams and sharks for three days and nights. By the time the American fleet realized the Indianapolis had been sunk and had sent rescue ships to find them, there were only 470 sailors left.

One was Skip, and he was whole, although, it took him many months to recover from the trauma and he was left with chronic diarrhea. He would joke about it because that was his style, but we could never tease him again, once we had heard the story. Before that night, we had razzed him hard about all kinds of things, like "Who was the 'crazy' screaming out in the middle of the night last night?" we asked. Or "Man, if we could have found him we'd have killed him!" or "Hey, who was that carrying on last night? Must have been some wild and crazy lovemaking. Whew, they ought to teach a course!"

Never again. We knew who it was and it was okay with us.

During the next three years we learned more about Normandy, Italy, Iwo Jima and Guadalcanal than people could handle. We couldn't, so we would weep for our husbands and wrap our arms around them...anything to ease the memories of battles.

Nesting

Before I was married, I had no idea that I was artistic or that I might possibly be a good cook.

After I was married, I started decorating with a vengeance (so Perk said). A lack of money slowed me down, but it didn't stop me. The cooking was another story.

After I painted the trailer door red, I knew, I needed something else if I wanted to give my doorway oomph. "I know," I said to myself, "I need a big container on each side of the door and some kind of tree in each one."

I pondered for days on where to find containers – free. Getting the trees would be easy. I'd just dig up long leaf pines in the wood, but the containers defeated me. Then a brilliant idea struck! I'd go to the fish market, cajole two wooden herring buckets out of the fish sellers. Then I'd take them home, paint them and plant them.

They looked at me rather oddly when I asked for buckets. "You want herring buckets?" I nodded. "You're sure?" nodded more vigorously. "O.K." They said reluctantly. "If you're sure."

Within a week, I got a call "Miz Perkinson, we got some herring buckets for you. You better pick them up soon 'cause they're kinda smelly." They were.

I smiled at Mr. Dross, the owner. "Can I rinse these with your hose please, I've got to take these home on the bus?"

"No'm, you sure don't want to do that…"

"Why?"

"It'll run everybody off the bus."

"No, no, I'm not going far, just to Copeley Hill," I reassured him.

"Well, it's your decision, Ma'am."

I rinsed the buckets well, let them drain carefully and headed for the bus stop. No problem. In an attempt to look casual, I stuck one bucket inside the other and carried them in my arms like new buckets. No problem. As I walked, I prayed they wouldn't smell. By the time I got to my stop, they were beginning to send up a small suggestion that something might recently have died in them, but before the passengers could pinpoint the problem, I was gone and that was that.

It took days to get the odor out of the buckets. Days of scrubbing, soaking and finally Chloroxing, before I could paint my treasures red and plant them and place them on either side of my steps. The combination of the dark gray trailer with the red door and red buckets was wonderful. However, there was a price to pay.

Several times, I had noticed the Copeley bus going by with its doors and windows open. "That's funny," I said, "it's freezing outside." The next day I noticed it again as the bus approached to pick passengers up. I was last in line, when suddenly Bud, the bus driver, slammed the door shut and drove off, leaving me dumbfounded. Needless to say, I had to walk to work.

That evening Bud asked me to step to the back of the line, so I could get on last and talk to him. I did what he asked, and as I stepped back, he slammed the door in my face and drove off. By now I was furious, yet I had an inkling Bud's behavior might have something to do with my herring buckets. By the time I got home, my neighbors were gathered outside laughing and talking with Perk. As I walked up I started fussing, "Bud is plain crazy. Do you know he left me stranded twice?"

"Boy, do we know!" They interrupted. "The whole Hill knows." They cracked up laughing.

"Knows what?" I asked testily.

"He says you're never riding his bus again. You almost got him fired for stinking up his bus. He had to hand scrub the whole bus inside and hose it down, and it's taking days to dry out and even at that..." they were laughing like a bunch of hyenas.

"Thelma, you crazy thing, the drippings from the buckets got into the cracks of the bus."

"It couldn't have been much." I interrupted.

"It doesn't take MUCH!" and with that they fell apart again.

I stood looking at the far horizon, then at the grass, and finally back at them. The full impact of what I had, indeed, done struck me. I grinned. And then I giggled. "Poor Bud."

It took several more days before Bud would let me on the bus. After that, I baked cakes and pies for him on all the holidays until I left Copeley Hill. Bud told that story about me and my herring buckets for years.

But, what the heck. A girl's gotta do what a girl's gotta do. Sometimes Perk found my decorating amusing, sometimes he didn't.

"I don't understand why this fixing stuff is so important," he'd say, shaking his head.

"It is . Home is where my," I stopped and tried again. "It's to give my heart a lift. Yours, too. And," I added thoughtfully, "it's so our friends will have a place to come into and feel the same way: Safe from the world. Like it's an oasis."

"Yeah, but most of our friends don't fix their's ."

"Some do; some don't." I replied. "I do. Look, Perk, you didn't have a mother that 'fixed.' She didn't know how. She had no talent, and she had no money. Honest to God, Perk, I don't mean that in an ugly way. It's just a fact.

"I was raised to think home was a place that was warm and safe and pretty." I continued, "It's fun making a home for the two of us, and it's fun finding I'm really good at it. Until I finish the trailer, I don't care about new clothes or makeup or anything like that. I'll do without it all. That gives me my weekly allowance to spend on the trailer."

Finally, our home was finished. Originally, it was a collapsible Army trailer. This meant the sides could be lifted up and enclosed, making a small square building with dry storage underneath and a bedroom area, living area, galley Kitchen and small bath and shower in the trailer itself. We heated with a kerosene stove.

But now, this small gray nonentity had become a charming cottage of greens and pink-check gingham and creams and brown. My materials came from Woolworth's, and I had found just the right furniture in junk stores. Everything was scaled down, of course, because it had to fit the trailer. Then, I had refinished or painted all the pieces. People who came into our home were always enchanted, and Perk seemed to be proud of that. But he never said much.

The norm on Copeley Hill was 'drab but functional.' The consensus seemed to be that you needed money to create beauty. No money, no beauty. Now and then, one of the young wives would accomplish such a feat by seeing pictures and pouring over the _American Home_ to learn how to be creative and persistent with the little money she had. I admired those women greatly. We couldn't help living poor, but we sure could help living ugly.

The final step in my trailer transformation was one I deliberately saved for last -- the floor. It was dark gray and ugly.

"Let's paint it!" I said. "Let's paint it dark green!"

"You're crazy," Perk said, "we'd have to move all the furniture OUT!"

"Un-unh – we could do it room by room."

"And how long will it take to dry?" Perk asked condescendingly. By now he was turned off to decorating.

"Maybe a couple of days. Hey, I've got an idea. We'll paint and put some bricks down and walk on those until it dries. Then...then," I continued hurriedly, "we'll paint where the bricks were!"

"I dunno." Perk shook his head.

"Look, Mamma said they'd buy the paint. But you're better at these things, so you talk to the paint store about this stuff called deck enamel."

And Perk did just that. He talked to the man about deck enamel, and he brought it home, and we painted half the trailer and walked on bricks for a few days.

'Two or three days' turned into a week. The paint was still tacky. Another week passed, and the paint was still tacky.

By now, our nerves were frazzled and our feet hurt. I threw the bricks out. "We'll just take our chances. If it's tacky, it's tacky." I said disgustedly.

That was where I made my mistake. The paint clung to our feet on the way to the bathroom. It stuck to Perk's shoes on the way to school. It relentlessly came up in jagged chunks – even after it dried.

"This is horrible, horrible," I moaned to Perk.

"Well, it was your dumb idea," he said, "Now you're stuck with it."

"Yes, but how did I know you didn't tell the man at the paint store we were painting linoleum?"

"I don't want to discuss it." Perk turned over in the bed. "We're just going to live with it!"

"For three more years?" I gasped.

No reply from Perk.

The next day, I stopped by the basement in Woolworth's. To be specific, I went to the linoleum section.

"Do you have layaway?" I asked the salesman.

"Yes, ma'am. And we're also having a sale."

"That'll help," I answered. "What have you got in green?"

With that, he pulled out a huge roll of green that was perfect. "You take the whole thing, I'll let you have it for six dollars."

I pondered a second and agreed. I promptly put fifty cents down. It took almost a month to pay off the layaway, but when it was time my buddy, Phil, the Copeley Hill maintenance man, picked it up in his truck and put it under our trailer in the enclosed storage space.

"Phil, please don't tell anyone. Especially Perk. He's going to kill me!" I begged. I was really nervous.

"Nope. Not a word. But he's got to know sooner or later."

"I know, but I've got to pick the time," I said. "Timing is everything..."

Each day we scraped paint off our feet and each day I resolved to tell him.

I came home from the studio one day to find Perk standing over the roll of linoleum in the rain – in a rage.

"What have you done? Where the hell did this come from?" he yelled.

"I bought it for six dollars out of our food money. It came from Woolworth's. I just couldn't stand it." I explained.

"Well, you can be sure I'm not putting this down! You must be crazy. Here I don't eat halfway decent, and you take it out of the food money," he raged.

"I don't eat halfway decent either," I said in a measured tone, "so you didn't put in but half! I put in the other half of not eating right. Besides, it's done. No more chipped paint." I said brightly, to calm things down.

"Why didn't you ask me?" he admonished me.

"You'd have said 'No'."

"Then 'No' it should have been!"

"No. It should not have been 'No'. It should have been 'let's see if we can figure out a way to do it'." I insisted. "I'm willing to share decisions, Perk, but you seem to downright enjoy saying 'no' when it could be 'yes', or 'let's talk about it'. I hate that! Well," I added quietly, " I guess you better get used to it 'cause I'm living half this marriage and the whole part of my life and if I decide it would be

'yes' now and then, and I can pay for it, that's what it's going to be."
By now we were both soaking wet from the rain.

"Not out of the food money," Perk persisted.

"Listen, Pickle Puss, I earn that food money," I reminded him.
"But, okay."

Perk turned and went into the trailer. I followed as he was
gathering up dry clothes and books. He knocked some paint chips
off his shoes then headed for the door.

"Where you going? We've got to put the linoleum up. I can't do
it alone, it's too heavy for me."

He looked at me and narrowed his eyes. "I'm not touching a
thing." Then he drove off.

Slowly I went down the steps and over to the huge roll. Tears of
frustration rolled down my cheeks and mixed with rain. I gritted my
teeth as I grabbed the roll. "Ugh..ugh..UGH!" I grunted at the top of
my voice. With the last huge grunt I slipped and fell full length into
the mud!

I managed to stand up and grab the huge roll again. **"UGH-H-
H,"** I grunted as I tugged. The linoleum started sliding, and as it
picked up momentum, my feet went out from underneath me and I
went into the mud again face down this time. At that moment Phil,
the maintenance man, drove by and slowed to a stop.

"What's going on?" He yelled as he eyed the linoleum.

Slowly I rolled over, propped my head up on my muddy hand
and hollered back, "What the Sam Hill do you think's going on?
Nothin!"

Phil broke into laughter so hard his face turned red.
w..aw..aw..AW..AW..AW!"

The idiot! Then he jumped out of his truck, still snorting and
snickering, and grabbed one end of the roll. The linoleum slid
smoothly into the space, out of the rain.

"Thanks, Phil. What would I do without you?" I was out of breath and panting.

"Was that Perk going down the road?" he asked quizzically.

"Yep."

"He was leaving this out?"

"Yep."

"Boy, I can't believe it." He looked at me for a long moment. "Hey...don't worry, the worst is over."

"How do you know?" I asked doubtfully.

"Okay..okay..haven't you got your flooring?"

"Well, yes."

"Haven't you got it paid for?"

"Yes..."

"Aren't I gonna put it down for you – free?"

"You are?"

"Yep! So look what you've accomplished. Perk got mad, okay, but you needed this floor and you got it. I'm proud of you!"

"You're proud of me?"

"Yep! Atta girl!" he grinned.

Phil got in his truck. "This week...it'll be in," he hollered as he drove off.

I stood in the cold rain for a long time looking at the drab gray trailers. Three hundred and fifty of them, row on row, as far as the eye could reach.

"So this is living," I said to myself over and over like a mantra, up the stairs and into my trailer. Atta girl. Atta girl...Atta...girl."

Royce & Harley

He beat her. He knocked her over a low brick wall. Then, he left for school in his car. "I told you to keep your mouth shut," he screamed.

Royce pulled herself together, redressed and drove to our trailer on Copeley. The special group of law students' wives was gathering to have a rare female-only party. Usually, someone's husband was home, studying; but this Saturday there was a conference at the Law School.

We'd come together for food and drink and outrageous conversation: sex methods, babies, food, gossip, with lots of laughter interspersed.

"Hey, Royce, you're sitting there awfully quiet."

Looking down I noticed a bruise and some swelling across both her lower legs. "Wow, what happened?"

Royce kept her voice calm. "Oh, I was chasing the dog and fell over the wall along the yard." They'd lived on Copeley for a short time, but then they moved to a cottage her mother rented for them.

Marge Boozer reached over to pull Royce's skirt aside. She gasped, "My god, Royce, you've got bruises all over your legs. You look like you're been kicked by a horse, honey!"

With that Royce burst into tears. "He beat me...Harley beat me..." She lifted her bangs to show a mean blow on the forehead.

"Oh my god, Royce, look at your arms." I gently pulled her sleeves up.

Jane Watson knelt in front of her and quietly said "Did he hit you in your stomach or chest?"

Royce nodded.

"Will you let me look?"

Royce nodded.

Jane lifted the blouse and we all openly flinched. There were huge black bruises the size of a fist.

"That S.O.B.!" Marge said, "Wait'll I tell Bill!"

"No, no, no" screamed Royce. "You can't! You can't tell anyone." She began to shake violently. I sat quietly for a moment then I said firmly "No one...no one will. You have my word. Right?" I looked at all six women.

Each one nodded.

"Your word?" They nodded.

"As soon as we've calmed down, we have to get you to Student Health."

"No" Royce replied. "It'll be all over school in twenty-four hours."

"Not if we do it my way," I said.

"What's your way?"

I grinned. "I call Student Health, tell her six of us have to see Dr. Emlaw right away and then all six of us go with Royce. When his nurse tells him that, he'll know something is up. I'm banking on him seeing us. That way no one person gives their name alone."

Everybody started whooping and laughing at the same time.

"You're one big nut, Perkinson!"

"Perfect!"

Within ten minutes we were walking into Student Health.

"Your name?" the nurse asked.

We all gave our name at one time.

"One at a time, one at a time," she demanded.

"No 'one at a time,'" I said. "We all go in together or we don't go. Call Dr. Emlaw...he'll say O.K."

She pursed her lips, disapprovingly, but she pushed his button. "Seven women are out here insisting you see them. Together."

"Seven of them?" he queried. "Well, send them in."

We walked in looking very purposeful.

"O.K." he said. "What's going on that I have to see seven ladies at one time?"

We turned to Royce. "Show him."

She pulled up her shirt and slowly turned around.

"Ohhh, honey. Who did this to you?" he demanded.

"My husband." Then she showed Dr. Emlaw her legs and arms and head.

We stood silently on one side of the room while he put her up on the table and treated the blows and scrapes methodically. He kept shaking his head and muttering under his breath. "I'll fix his wagon!"

"Harley can't find out..nobody can," Royce said fearfully. "He'll hurt me again!"

"You have my word," Dr. Emlaw said. "You ladies came in with her to cover, right?"

"Un-huh."

"So now, how are you going to get her out of town and to her home?" he asked. "She can not go back to that man. I will call her family and tell them she's coming..." He turned to Royce. "You are going home now. No clothes, no nothing... You are out!"

"I'll drive her," I said. "I have time to go down and back and Perk will never know."

With that, we left and took the girls to the trailer. Then Royce and I headed for the interstate.

Once I settled Royce, with her family, and put some food into my system I headed for Charlottesville myself reviewing the entire amazing, dreadful day. I'd never heard of any man beating his wife, much less a supposed "Virginia Gentleman."

But playing across my mind again and again was Dr. Emlaw's reaction to the abuse.

"He is going to do something...I know it...! I'm going to try to talk to him." I headed the car for Student Health.

"You back again?" Dr. Emlaw asked, surprised. "What's on your mind Miss Ma'am?"

"I got worried on the way back. I just know you are getting ready to so something about all this. I can tell! That's why I came straight here."

"Hunh! You can, huh?" With that he walked over to his desk and handed me a letter he had written.

When I saw how it started out: "you son of a bitch"

I knew I needed to sit down! It continued...

I saw you beat your wife today. I saw you knock her over a wall and drive off. I've checked your record and know you are a law student. And, of course, I know you were in the service. Me, too. Bouganville, Marines. And you can bet your ass I know some mean military procedures.

So here it is, you bastard: Not only will I be watching you, several of my buddies are going to take on the chore, too. As long as you are in Charlottesville, you will not touch another woman. I will personally see to that.

You'll be watched. Constantly. If I had been able to get to you before you drove off, I would have beaten you to a bloody pulp.

Remember.

I looked at Dr. Emlaw and asked, "Are you crazy? He'll check out every Marine in the city!"

He gave a snort, "Won't do any good. I wasn't in the Marines!" Then he really laughed.

I laughed too. Really laughed.

No one ever knew this story but Dr. Emlaw and me, and we knew why Harley was never quite the same! He was nervous -- kind of jumpy. People didn't seem to notice, but we did. One of our greatest joys was to watch Harley sweat whenever we brought Royce's name up (a lot!) and expressed sincere puzzlement at her leaving him "like that."

Royce divorced Harley and eventually married an wonderful older man. He was a UVA graduate and lawyer.

Harley went on to practice law. He developed a reputation for being an ill-mannered brute and a ruthless lawyer, who practiced just inside the letter of the law.

We were not surprised. Nor were we surprised to learn his second wife left him several years later.

The Law School of the University of Virginia took great pride in their reputation for graduating men of principle and honor.

Harley wasn't one of them.

Summertime, Summertime

The lazy, hot days of summer always began with a malevolent humidity that would settle down on Charlottesville and gradually change the rhythm of the little town. We went from the lively bustle of a college town to a sleepwalk cadence.

The open meadows that held Copeley Hill shimmered in the heat, and the trailers shimmered back - slowly becoming infernos that drove one out in the daytime, and left one limp and sleep deprived at night.

Those of us that owned fans treasured them even though they really didn't cool. Rather, a fan gathered hot air into an oscillating breeze that could dry off the perspiration.

No one had air conditioning. We never even experienced that miracle until Miller and Rhodes, Richmond's elegant department store, installed a system in 1952. Lowe's Theatre and Thalhimer's Department Store followed, and before long summers became manageable all over the South.

But Copeley Hill was another world. It moved in a mind-set and time frame that set it apart from the rest of the country.

Our little trailer was 20' x 20' and had a living room down one whole side, an entrance and a galley kitchen in the middle and a bedroom and tiny bath that flanked the rear. Front door, back door and seven small high windows that cranked out were our only ventilation - plus a ceiling vent that could also be cranked open. We had an icebox in our galley kitchen that had three doors. One outside, so the ice man could put the ice in; one opened inside so we could take food out; and another opened so we could chop off pieces of ice. Even with the heat, there were definite joys to summer. The husbands found jobs and left at nine and came home at five; others worked eight to four, or six to three like Perk and Pres Luck.

During the summer the Hill settled into a light-hearted, noisy place. For a time we were simply young couples with a right to exuberance. We pooled our money for kegs of beer; we pooled our money for extravagant steaks, and we made love and a lot of babies.

Perk and Pres heard that the stone quarry was paying high wages for dynamite blasters. So, egged on by each other, they applied for and got the jobs. Each day they worked like dogs in a relentless sun that heated the sheet stone cliffs to boiling.

They ran trip hammers for three days and blasted with dynamite for two, arriving home all five days grimy and exhausted. To make matters worse, the two blasting days brought severe headaches and wrenching nausea whenever the boys found themselves downwind from the fumes. Sometimes, Pres and Perk would manage to make it home before they threw up. More often than not, they'd toss their vittles out the car window on the journey home!

Thankfully, sympathetic and kindly neighbors washed down targeted spots along the way without complaint. Finally, we all just stood by with jugs of water on Tuesday and Thursday afternoons and kept our children were away from the curbs! The rest of the time the boys were fine.

During the war, many people had planted Victory Gardens. The University continued the tradition and set aside large areas for Copeley Hill. Perk signed up for us, and he proved to be an excellent gardener. His parents had always gardened and canned so he knew exactly what to grow and how to grow it. Together, we planted and watered and weeded and picked and canned.

We loved the abundance of fresh vegetable we'd grown ourselves; and we loved sharing with our friends. Incredibly, those who chose not to garden were careful to never ask for vegetables or to touch our gardens. The gardeners shared produce all summer with the non-gardeners and then, almost imperceptibly, the non-gardeners began to take over the job of watering the gardens. One by one gardening became the task of everyone. I loved that.

We were, for the most part wonderful cooks. Our exchanged recipes should have been collected into one book, a national treasure we could have called American Southern Gourmet. A meal of fresh string beans simmered for hours with a small ham hock, cold biscuits, and sweetened ice tea clinking with big chunks of ice chopped off the block in the icebox. Cucumbers and green onions soaked for several hours in salt water, drained and dressed with a few chunks of ice, vinegar and salt and pepper. Fried chicken cooked in butter and a little lard, gravy made with cream off the top of the milk bottle, mashed potatoes with lots of butter and lots of pepper and, finally, thick slices of tomatoes. As long as the strawberries lasted we made shortcake from long strips of pie crust sprinkled liberally with sugar, baked, then broken, to make layers of crust, cream and berries, crust, cream and berries...sometimes we used sugar biscuits instead of pie crusts.

Our group acquired a reputation throughout the Hill for our specialties. Hawk Watkins was famous for her three-squash casserole with fried bacon bits and nutmeg; Jane Watson, for her pound cake (a pound of everything!) with sherry. Mo was noted for her baked beans with bourbon pork chops tucked under the beans to bake, and Mickey Luck did an outrageous ham poached in cheap wine.

I made cole slaw with a special made-up dressing and caraway seeds, chicken salad with white grapes, and a knockout tomato aspic. Mary Francis Sims' meatloaf was beef and pork and whole hard-boiled eggs pushed down in the center over which she slathered homemade ketchup, and then baked. Her homemade refrigerator rolls were a treasure, and her congealed salads were four layers high.

Our "Summer Tournament for Badminton Balls and Boys & Girls" began in a quiet desperation to fill our time in the evenings. Before it was over for the summer, it had burgeoned into a source of fun and camaraderie for the whole Hill.

As soon as the sun went down, the badminton court was set up in the wide grass lawns between the trailer rows. Once a week, after grass cutting, the chalk boundaries were marked in the grass. Then we stretched the badminton nets each evening.

Participants signed up for each set and neighbors would bring out standing lamps on extension cords to light the court. They also brought out chairs to sit in along the viewing section.

"Lively" might be an appropriate word, but "raucous" probably came closer to describing the games on Friday and Saturday nights.

We drank iced tea in gallons and ate watermelons and spat out the seeds with great pleasure.

Participation in the games increased dramatically each week. Finally we moved to have the games six nights a week, but lights were out by ten on week nights and eleven on weekends.

In those days, children could sleep through anything, so that was not a problem. The grownups played and cheered outside and the kids were dead-to-the-world inside. If they needed us, we were nearby.

The fun was every night for everyone. The guys were great at badminton; but it was the girls who turned into tigers on the courts and beat the socks off the men.

These evenings were pure joy, a reprieve from the long months of school, tests, forced solitude, and studying or tiptoeing around someone who had to study.

As the months went by, the number of spectators increased because the badminton games became more and more exciting and more outrageous. Not only were the players outstanding to watch, their "uniforms" got funnier and funnier.

The men played in their wives' high-heels and often their hats. The wives would come out "en masse" wearing their husbands' boxer shorts (which hung to their knees) and UVA ties.

We spent the summer trying to out do each other's costumes but the men won hands down. They arrived - all of them - for the tournament play-offs wearing their wives' long girdles with the stocking tabs – the clips that held up the hosiery - hanging down. Short socks and sneakers completed the outfits.

They made sure the crowd was waiting. Then they marched solemnly from between the trailers, led by an honor guard banging buckets with huge kettle spoons.

After the tournament winners had been acknowledged and duly crowned with wreaths made of linked hot dogs, nets were taken down and the chairs moved back. Large galvanized washtubs were brought out and filled with our beloved Purple Passion made from gin, grape juice and huge blocks of ice...all donated by the Copeley Hill Market.

Food was put out on the table - donated by each trailer - radios were coordinated on the same station, and the dancing began....

During our summers, the music could play, the doors could bang, and conversations could ebb and flow, at will with people who came and went freely.

We began to look young again. All of us.

From the Vinegar Hill to Pungmonyung

"...From Vinegar Hill to Rugby Road we're gonna get drunk tonight..." UVA College Song

From the first moment we arrived at the University of Virginia, we all, men and women, resolved to do anything and everything we could to get the men through school – financially or otherwise.

"I know a way to make fifteen bucks a month easy," Perk informed me one evening over dinner. Dinner was stuffed franks and salad.

The recipe had been sent to me by the best cook in Tupelo, Mississippi, the mother of Charles "Mississippi" Inzer. He was a single student and a favorite of ours. The recipe consisted of chopped hot dogs, green peppers, olives, onion, cheese, chili sauce, mustard and mayonnaise stuffed into a hot-dog roll, wrapped in Reynolds Wrap, then baked. The dish was simple, and so good everybody on Copeley Hill wanted the recipe. I wouldn't give it to them. If I had, I would have had to eat my own food at other peoples' trailers! I didn't give out Mrs. Inzer's other wonderful recipes either, for the same reason. I just said they were family recipes. Of course, I was including myself and Charles Inzer's relatives in the same large Southern family.

"Did you hear me?" Perk asked.

I swallowed. "Fifteen dollars? How?"

"I join the Marine Corps Reserves. I go to meetings two nights a month, and I get fifteen bucks!" He stood there, grinning.

"Do it! I mumbled, wiping away the wonderful drippings from my sandwich. "Fifteen dollars will feed us for two weeks."

It seemed such a good idea that boys from the University, as well as the 'Townies', signed up in large numbers, swelling the ranks of the Marine reserves until Charlottesville could boast the second largest reserve group in Virginia..

With the privilege of being a Marine came the requirement to wear the uniform. Perk summarily removed his uniform and hat from the closet and wore them to each meeting.

At first, I thought he was really handsome in his uniform. He was so lean and so masculine in the khaki green uniform with its double row of gleaming buttons down his front. But by the fifth or sixth moth, I found I did not like for him to even put it on. There was something ominous about it. No matter what I told myself, the feeling persisted. I was frightened.

"How do I look?" He'd ask, strutting about in his uniform.

"You look o...kay," I'd answer, a little flatly.

"Okay? You used to say I looked great."

"I know." I'd smile.

"Then what's the matter?"

"I don't know, honey. I get down right shivery when I see you in it. It's like a voice warning me, and I can't figure out why."

As fate would have it, my studio began to make more money. Perk became more and more engrossed in school, and the Marine Reserve and the uniform became less important.

"Get out of the Reserves," I encouraged Perk. "We don't need the money, and you need the time. Just resign," I said over and over.

"Okay, okay, I'll resign next week." A week later, he did. But he failed to return his uniform.

I'd forget it was in his closet. Then I'd move a piece of clothing to hang up shirts I'd just ironed and

suddenly see it. Each time, the sense of foreboding returned.

"Perk, take the uniform back. You're not out of the Reserves until you take it back."

"I will...I will!"

"Now!"

"I will!"

"Tonight, please honey, tonight!"

"Okay...Tonight!"

"You promise?"

"Ye, Gods!"

"Promise?"

"Okay, I promise." And he did. Finally, he was officially out of the Marines; and my fears eased.

One evening, in late winter, I came home from work and stood looking up at my trailer. I loved its red door and ruffled curtains. I loved the lights glowing cozily inside. I softly said a litany of blessings: we had each other, we were safe and school was going all right.

"Hey, hon." Perk looked pale as I opened the door.

The trailer was filled with eight or ten of the husbands. They were so quiet – so pale. There were no smiles. Something was obviously wrong.

"What? What is it?" I asked softly.

No one spoke.

"What is it?" I asked again.

"We can't tell you."

"Has someone died?" I was terrified, but didn't let on.

"No."

"Then why can't you tell me?" I was calm. I wanted to reassure them that I could handle anything.

"Thelma, you'll have to trust me on this," Perk said quickly.

I looked at him for a long moment. "I can do that." I walked back into the galley Kitchen. "I'm fixing tea.

I'll turn on the radio, and you can talk without my hearing you. But in ten minutes, we will all stop talking and have a wonderful hot cup of tea." My eyes searched their faces.

"Together – and count our blessings. Most especially ... especially will give thanks for the young wives on this hill who are home cooking dinner.

"Good Lord," I said to myself as I went into the Kitchen, "that was really sappy." Then, in the next moment, I thought, "Maybe not, this is what women do best." I turned the stove on for tea.

All through the evening husbands came and went, talking outside the trailers. The next morning before

school, the same thing took place. Interestingly, there were no wives visible in the groups, nor was there conversation of any kind among them about the strange goings on.

Perk was waiting for me when I got home that evening from work.

"Well, hon, where are we with developments whatever they are?" I asked him.

"You remember how you carried on about the Marine Reserves?"

"...and nearly drove you crazy about the uniform?" I said, half smiling. "I never could figure out why I got so obsessed about all that."

Perk walked over and put his arms around. "Well, I know why, I also know you have saved me from something terrible. Maybe even losing my life."

I turned to search his face. "You're serious."

"Yes, I am serious. The Marine Corps Reserve is shipping out for Korea tonight."

56

Disbelief became a knot in my stomach. "How do you know? They've already been to war. They can't take them again, can they?" The icy feeling was back.

"Yes, they can," Perk said firmly, "They are *bona fide* of the United States Marine Corps Reserve. And," he said angrily, "they're taking them. America is going to war!"

"All for fifteen dollars a month," I replied, flatly.

"Wait a minute how do you know this? Surely this is a secret or something..." My eyes searched his face, looking for a small sign of doubt. It wasn't there.

"It's a military secret, and you're right. We aren't supposed to know. We also know none of these guys are allowed to call their families to tell them what's happening."

"So, they can't even say goodbye?" I asked, sadly.

"That's it."

"And it's like they just disappear with nobody knowing?"

"Well, no, not exactly," Perk said slowly, "we're going to the train station tonight."

I was puzzled.

"The unit's train leaves at 9:15 p.m., and we're going to be there." Perk explained.

"All of us?"

He looked at me with an odd expression...like he was resolved to take care of those Marines...to be there to tell them goodbye. They were, clearly, his brothers.

"Yes. All of us." He paused. "When we get there, you're not to say a word. You are not to acknowledge anyone, not our friends, not the Marines we know..."

"And we just stand there?" I questioned.

"Just stand there," he stated matter-of-factly. "No one is to wave, for any reason," he continued.

"Why are we doing that? Why can't we show them how we feel?" I was becoming outraged. "That's stupid!."

"Easy…" Perk said softly. "We cannot signify in any way, Thelma. This is a military secret. Do you understand what that means? Frankly, how the Hell it got out I don't know. At first we argued about it, but I'll be damned if these guys are going back to war without us being there at that station when they pull out."

His voice broke. "They're not coming back. Not a damn one of them. Do you know that? Do..you..know..that?" He hammered his fist on the table next to him. "They'll be killed or be cut up..or freeze to death." He was sobbing, deep wrenching sobs, "Ohhh GOD!" He put his forehead down on the table and cried for a very long time.

The evening was miserable: Perk couldn't study; I couldn't seem to get dinner on – just some soup, which we couldn't eat; we couldn't even talk. The sadness moved out of the trailer with us into the car.

The cars that lined University Drive on the way to the station that night were full of people; yet everyone was so still. The slanting raindrops blown by a high mountain wind provided the only animation.

Another long line of headlights came out of the University grounds. It converged with the headlights of cars from Copeley Hill. All of the cars were dark, each appearing to follow its own headlights through slicing rain.

We wondered how all the traffic would manage to park at the train station without a small catastrophe.

Incredibly, the police were there with shielded lights, guiding us with small silent motions into order.

Several hundred professors and students, their wives and people from the town gathered on the station platform without making a sound. No one spoke. Everyone waited. The night was bitter, and the fog flumed up, distorting our shapes and faces in the dim lights.

We heard the sound of softly marching feet move toward the station platform, toward us. As the troops neared, we stepped back creating a wide path for the soldiers of the Marine Corps Reserve of Charlottesville, Virginia, U.S.A. They were dressed in khaki uniforms, and they bore the heavy weight of huge backpacks.

They were leaving us, their school, and their America.

As I looked into their faces, I realized I was looking into the faces of soldiers, not students, not boys. Their faces held layers of knowing, fear, the horror of memory. They had been to war before. They knew. An instant had removed them from the world of football games and proms, frat parties and trailer doors.

As we stood peering through the windows at guarded faces peering back at us, the train pulled away. I raised my hand and then my arm. We all did. We couldn't help it.

We held our frozen wave until the train disappeared from sight. Then, we wept. We couldn't help it.

The Marine Corps Reserve of Charlottesville was overwhelmed by the North Koreans at Pungmonyung. Those who were not killed, froze to death in the year 1950, in that first dreadful winter of the Korean War.

The Last Time I Saw Paris

Captain Francis Beauregard Carter and his beautiful wife Cynthia, who looked like a model, lived four trailers Down from us. His family was New Orleans French and Virginia aristocracy; but, to his credit, he tried to stand on his own two feet.

Beau was held in high esteem by all who knew him. Because of his clarity of thought his professors admired him. Because of his ability to help his men on Copeley who developed proxyms of "the shakes" or had kaleidoscopes of nightmares troubled with arms, legs, shrapnel, blood and screams flying through the air, he was valued.

For the men, he had character. For his professors, he had character. For himself, his wife and his marriage, he had little.

The veterans recognized a missing space in him - a deadness within his own personal world - and they knew better than to bring it up. They had tried.

Beau Carter walked his friends through sadness, reassuring them, "We cleaned up those monsters, and now everybody's safe. If you can't trust that, it's all wasted. You know what I mean? I know how you feel, but all the blood and guts weren't a loss." When Carter spoke, the nerves, the shakes, and the nightmares would subside.

In gatherings away from the Carters, there was often speculation about how long Cynthia would stay with Beau, or how long he could continue before his own demons exploded.

A new couple, the Smithfields, moved into the trailer directly across from the Carters. They were a stunning, charming, newlywed couple, and all the hill fell in love with them. The husband, Duncan, was pre-med and witty. He had marched into Paris with the American Army of Occupation. His wife, Monique, was French (a Parisian!) and divine. She was the love of all the Smithfields: Duncan, his family, and half of Smithfield, Virginia.

One Saturday the couples began to gather at our trailer. One couple stopped by bringing drinks for themselves, then another, and then more. Finally, as often happened, a party began. We decided to walk down to the Smithfield's and invite them to join us. We would initiate them to the Party Customs of Copeley Hill.

On the way someone yelled, "Hey, Beau! Come on over." The door opened to the Carter's trailer.

"What?"

"Come..on..over." We yelled in one voice.

"Okay, let me get Cynthia." Beau went back into the trailer.

"And a drink!" We yelled back.

"We haven't met them yet," Monique said.

"You'll like them," we reassured her.

Cynthia and Beau approached with smiles on their lips and Purple Passions in their hands.

We introduced them. "Cynthia and Beau, this is Duncan and Monique Smithfield." Everything was relaxed and normal until Monique spoke. "Ah, your first name is Frank? This is *Francois* French." She spoke with a lilting French accent. "So I will call you '*Francois*'."

As she turned to acknowledge Cynthia, Frank whispered, "I'll be right back." He bolted, and he didn't come back.

The rest of us, including Cynthia, got into the rhythm of the lazy fall Saturday afternoon. Conversations ebbed and flowed, as did the alcohol, and gradually, the food and blankets began to appear. We partied all evening between the trailers, the way we always did on Copeley Hill.

The weeks that followed passed uneventfully. There was little to talk about except school and Beau. He was noticeably paler, thinner, and more somber. Something was definitely working on Beau and it wasn't good. The men of Copeley recognized demons when they saw them. So they decided to take him down to one beer joint near the University and loosen him up. It would be a 'guys' night out on the town.

Surprisingly Beau agreed, and even more surprisingly, he relaxed and began to talk about the war.

"I didn't bargain for this," Pres Luck whispered to Perk.

"Me, either," complained Armpy Dye, who was seated next to him.

"Who'd we do this for?" asked Perk. "Us or him?"

"Him," they chorused.

"Okay, so let's go to work on him." said Pres.

"What do you mean?"

"We ask him questions and pull him out. Let's find out what's really eating him."

"Right. So you start, Pres. You're more mature about this stuff," Perk suggested.

Pres thought for a moment. "Beau, where were you during the war?"

Beau looked up from his beer. "Europe." His voice was flat.

"Beginning, middle or end?" Armpy asked.

"Beginning...middle...and end."

"Normandy?"

Beau nodded. "Towns, tanks, bazookas, grenades, flame throwing through France, then over to Holland and into Germany." He reached for his beer. "I lost two complete units, half of another, and I began to shake so that I couldn't hold a gun steady. They moved me back to a unit that was in a pincer movement heading deep into France toward Paris."

"Did you get to Paris?"

"Yep, I got to Paris."

"How come you never mentioned it or told the Smithfields when you met them?"

Beau replied, "I don't talk about Paris much."

"Great God, man, you're a walking damn miracle!" Bill Boozer breathed. "Most of the guys that landed on Normandy were killed or wounded. Those crazy generals sent in green recruits. The ones that got through Normandy were finished off in the European battles.

"That's right." Beau's voice wavered. "But some of us made it. Only thing is, two years into the war I was beginning to fight alongside guys whose brothers and friends had been killed in the first waves, and now they were taking their places. They were too young for the first draft, but they sure as hell were old enough by then. By then, they were old men of eighteen and nineteen."

One by one, the eight veterans at the table nodded.

"I was eighteen."

"I was nineteen."

"Me, too, but I was in the Pacific."

"Iwo Jima?"

"Naw, Leyte, Guam, the Philippines."

"Well, at least you didn't get everything you had frozen from frost bite in temperatures so cold you could hardly pee."

"Naw, I got foot rot, jungle fever, fungus and malaria instead, you jerk."

"Gentlemen, gentlemen." Bill interrupted. He turned to Beau. "Tell us what it was like marching into Paris. I've seen newsreels, but my God, it must have been one glorious experience after what you'd been through."

Beau sat for a moment, clearly moving back through time. "I'm going to tell you guys a story," he said, "but you gotta swear that you will never tell! Never."

The young men gathered around him nodding their promise.

"Paris," he began, "is the most beautiful city in God's world, I'm telling you. The Germans didn't bomb it because they meant to save it for themselves...not for the world, for themselves. And thank God they did!"

The men sat quietly, as if he were handing them the key to the city.

"I marched into Paris with tears running down my face. We all did."

"What about the French?" asked Armpy.

"My God, they went crazy." Beau grinned for the first time. "Can you imagine a million people wanting to kiss you?" He paused. "Okay, I'm going to tell you something I've never told anyone."

"I was marching in the formation, and I saw this girl standing close to the curb. She looked like something out of a picture in a museum. Not knockdown gorgeous, but that French look that can grab your heart in a minute. It's so, so feminine and chic, and so mysterious and enchanting. French women can be beautiful without being beautiful, I'll tell you."

He lit a cigarette and took a deep gulp of his beer. The men sat silently, waiting.

"Well," he continued, "we marched past her, and two blocks later, there she was again at the curb watching me go by. At first I though she was just following the crowd, but when it happened again several blocks later, I told myself, 'Something is going to happen here.' "

"We marched on to the end of the boulevard and broke formation. All of a sudden, there she was again. Nanette Bouzier." He shook his head in remembered wonderment.

"Great God Almighty!" someone said.

"Yes. She was just that," replied Beau. "She walked up to me, slipped her hand into mine and said, 'I'm Nanette. I have no family to celebrate with. I will make you my family. Her English was pretty good!"

"Weren't you worried that she was a prostitute?" asked Bill.

"Christ Almighty Man! Have you lost your mind?" Beau laughed out loud. "Who would've cared?"

The crowd dissolved in laughter.

"Well, she turned out to be everything a man dreams of. She wasn't a prostitute, but we did make love in her funny little flat with a balcony. It was located on the Left Bank, and had thin white curtains hanging to the floor in front of French doors. They blew a little in the breeze. I can't tell you," Beau stated, "how French and sexy those sheer curtains were!"

The men sat mesmerized. "So," Perk finally asked, "what happened to Nanette?"

"I left her," Beau said.

"What?"

"I promised to come back for her, but I didn't. My family, my friends, school, all took Nanette's place. Then I met Cynthia and married her."

"Just like that?" someone asked.

"Just like that. And the minute I did it, I knew I'd made the mistake of my life leaving France, leaving Nanette."

"Do you know what happened to her?" Perk asked.

"No," he said sadly, "I contacted her concierge finally and found out that she'd moved out. So I rented her little apartment, and I've kept it waiting there ever since with both our names on the nameplate next to the door."

"Just sittin' empty?"

Beau nodded.

"What does Cynthia say about this?"

"She doesn't know."

"She doesn't know about Nanette?"

"No, but she suspects something. She keeps asking me where I'm at. That drives me crazy, because I'm always with Nanette. Those days with her haunt me." He sighed, "It isn't fair to Cynthia, and I don't know what to do about it. It's a mess."

"So what'll you do if you ever find this French girl?"

"Oh, God," Beau groaned. "I ask myself that over and over."

"What's the answer?"

"I'd leave and go to her."

"Let me ask you something," Armpy said, leaning over the table to get a closer look at Beau. "What is it that obsesses you so?"

"Have you ever marched into Paris and found an intelligent, lovely young French woman asking you to be her family?" Beau was getting defensive. "...who had suffered and known terror and starvation, who had no one to care? She'd lost her entire family. No one was left to care if she lived or died."

"No," they shook their heads.

"Damned right," Beau continued, "and the minute we began to make love, I knew I had come all the way through the war to save her. It was like my soul melted into hers."

"All I wanted to do," he continued, "was to put her in a palace, dress her in silks and diamonds and make her world perfect."

"You know what she said?" Beau asked his audience. "She said I had. She said there really are knights in shining armor and I was one of them." He shook his head in disbelief.

66

"And you came back without her?" Pres asked, dumbfounded.

Beau nodded miserably.

"And you never sent for her," Pres said flatly. He paused, "You know, something is wrong here. How come Duncan could marry Monique, but you couldn't marry Nanette? How come?"

Beau looked past him, getting upset. "I don't know."

"Yes, you do. You know," Pres insisted, "you know and won't admit it."

"If you're so damn smart, suppose you tell me." Beau snapped.

"It's all the Beauregard stuff and the Carter stuff, it's ...it's snobbery.

Beau sat back stunned.

"You're not a knight in shining armor, you're a 'Beau regard'. You're not a brave young lover in a brave new world, you're ... you're a 'Carter'!"

"Hold it!" Pres thrust out his hand. "Don't interrupt! I'm going to finish. I'm from Clinch Valley, the Virginia coal mines. I'm the first ever in my family to go to college, Beau. But I'm more generous of spirit toward myself and my fellow man that you'll ever be. You're a half dead man who survives fighting all the way through Europe, helping to save the world, and then, heads right back to be safe at the country club."

"Whoa!" yelled Bill Boozer, "That's it! That's as far as anyone goes."

Beau jumped to his feet, sending his chair crashing over as he shouted, "You're a liar, a stupid jackass liar. It was none of those things. And you," he leveled an outraged look at Pres, "are the snob!"

"Simple, underprivileged 'you' have moved up, haven't you? Now you're automatically above anyone who was privileged or had an 'easy life'. You try to make me out to be the snob, while all the time it's you."

"And the reason I left her," Beau said, taking a deep breath, determined to see this through, "was that she was a collaborator."

"A what?" asked Perk.

"A collaborator. She had fraternized with the Germans." Beau answered numbly.

"Jesus, man, how'd you find that out?" Parlier asked.

Beau had calmed himself, straightened his chair, and sat down. "I got an early weekend pass, and I hurried to reach the apartment to surprise Nanette, but I was nervous, you know? Like something was wrong."

"I rounded the corner and there, straight ahead of me in the courtyard, was a crowd holding three women and screaming and spitting at them and hitting them with their fists."

"They had shaved the head of one of the women." Beau shook his head in disbelief. "It was Nanette, and she was crying and screaming and trying to cover her head with her hands. I thought it was so odd to see her do that - to cover her head and just let the blows fall without trying to fend them off."

"God, Beau," Frank Watkins said quietly.

"Yeah," he answered.

"What did you do?"

"I walked across that street, shoved the crowd aside, daring them to hit me or spit on me. Then I got Nanette out of there. She was shaking so hard I had to carry her. She couldn't stand up for hours, almost the whole day."

"What happened to the other women?" asked Pres. By now he'd forgotten the insults they had hurled at one another.

"Honest to God," said Beau. "The crowd shaved their heads and beat them to a bloody pulp."

"You know what I did?" Beau asked. "I went down with an unloaded German Lugar I'd bought as a souvenir, stood in the doorway and yelled at the top of my voice, 'I'm counting to five, and if you're not out of here, I'm shooting. One, Two..' Those disgusting, smelly Frenchies flew." Beau burst out laughing. "I mean they were *fighting* get out of that courtyard."

"What happened to the other two women?"

"I took them up to the apartment, fixed them up, gave them a brandy, made beds on the floor for them and told them to sleep. No one was going to hurt them while I was there."

Perk looked at Beau wide-eyed. "You had three beaten female collaborators sleeping in the apartment, and you were their guardian? Unbelievable!"

"All that night I sat up wondering how their lives had come to this, and watching out the windows for more trouble."

"And?" Perk said.

"Strange thing is," Beau answered, "the American soldiers had heard a lot about collaborators. Half of Paris had hobnobbed with the Germans, dining and dancing at the Ritz, being entertained by the top singers and entertainers of France - Edith Piaf, Maurice Chevalier, on and on, movie stars, musicians."

"For some reason, because Marshall Petain was French and a Nazi puppet, and because he said it was okay, and because the Germans were ordered to act like gentlemen by Hitler, the French bought it. Not all of them, but a lot."

"Now the French patriots were punishing those who had betrayed their country."

"So I thought and thought about it and then I told her, 'Just because we're men doesn't mean we haven't been through hell and terror and misery. Am I wrong to expect a woman to have honor? To be true to her country? Other French women did. Why didn't you?'"

"What did she say?" asked Perk.

"She had no explanation. And I just stood there, looking at her. Finally, I said, 'Nanette, I will tell you one thing I know to be true: there would have been no American collaborators, no American entertainers betraying their homeland.' I packed my gear and at the door I turned and said, 'I believe I've had enough of the French. When I think of the lives it took to free you and your country...' and left."

"And now you can't forget her," said Parker.

"And now I can't forget her," repeated Beau. "And I can't forgive myself for not realizing that it was not so simple as I made it out."

"I'm going home." Beau wobbled a bit as he stood up.

"We're all going home," said Perk.

Days passed uneventfully after the boys' night on the town although it took the men days to recover. Their wives went on about life without comment; and for that, the men were grateful.

Then, Francis Beauregard Carter's darker side surfaced for all the world to see. He disappeared.

When Cynthia Carter found his note, she fell apart so badly that Dr. Ellerson had to come to her trailer and give her a shot to quiet her.

Beau wrote that he was leaving school. He said he was taking half their savings, and he was going back to Europe. He did not plan to come back.

All of us helped Cynthia with the packing. No rush, the University said. We took advantage of the time to talk truths and wisdom to her. Early on, we had a blanket party and decided to tell her where and why *Francois* gone. If she was going to heal, she needed to know the truth.

A week later she went home to her family. We never heard from her again. We called and left messages but she never called back. It was as though she had erased Copeley Hill from her life.

The Shack

It was hard to earn money in Charlottesville when we were there in 1949, 1950, and 1951. There were so few jobs. There weren't many places to live either. This country built nothing during the depression and World War II, so there were no apartments or houses to spare.

Until we could get a vacancy on Copeley hill, we all lived anywhere we could. Our friends, Russ and Andreena lived in a construction shack outside of town. The Parlier twins lived in a garage.

Fortunately, we found an unheated apartment on Vinegar Hill but we had to share the bathroom with the woman across the hall who sold her wares herself and bootleg whiskey seven days a week. It was unnerving because her customers often mistakenly beat on our door. Still, we were lucky. Even if we did have to heat water on the stove for our baths and wash our clothes on a scrub board in the bathtub, we had a home. Then, our name came up on the list for a trailer on Copeley Hill. Thank God! However, because we were desperate for money. Perk got the idea to peddle sandwiches at night to the students living in the new dormitory. Since there was no place to get a snack within two miles, and since the students didn't have cars, it was a natural. There were certainly no vending machines.

We began by buying a little Chevy roadster for $16.00 per month. We planned to use it to carry drinks and sandwiches to the dorm at night. We sold out the first night. We added Moon Pies. They sold out. Everything sold out every night!

"What do you think about a shack – a shack for sandwiches, drinks, candy and stuff?" Perk looked up from his books.

"A shack." I repeated his words.

"A shack," he repeated. "I'm serious. Look, they're building three more freshman dorms, right?"

"Right."

"The construction workers have gotta eat..."

"Right."

"How's about bringing someone in to help me run it, probably a law student. We can split 50/50 and go with it?"

"Who's going to build the shack? How're we going to pay for it? The University will never let you do that!"

Perk looked at me quietly. I could see a plan taking form in his head. "I'm going to Darden!"

"The President!" I was floored.

"I'm going to Darden. This week! We've got to have more money. Your piano studio is slow. The $75.00 government check won't cut it. We've got to have more." His voice stopped.

"I know." I said sadly. Then I said, "It's brilliant! Go see what you can do."

And he did. That apple-cheeked country boy hustled himself off to an appointment with the President of the University of Virginia regarding an important matter: The Shack. He would say that the students and construction workers needed it.

As Perk entered the office for his interview, President Darden stood up to shake his had and said, "Mr. Perkinson, I believe you've been in my office before."

Perk grinned and said, "I believe you're right sir."

"How's that little lady? How's Copeley Hill?" The older man asked.

"She's fine sir. Have you seen all the doors on Copeley Hill?" Perk grinned again.

"Indeed yes! I have to tell you, it's one of my wife's and my favorite little stories. We tell this one to visitors and foreign dignitaries and invariably have to take them to see for themselves." Darden leaned forward. "Now what can I do for you?" His eyes twinkled. "How's the Mayor of Copeley Hill doing, by the way?"

"He's doing fine, Mr. Darden." The grin was back, bigger than ever. "I'm Mayor of Copeley Hill now, sir." Perk said.

President Darden threw his head back and laughed uproariously. "My word, but you two are something! Wait'll I tell my wife." He paused.

Perk spoke up quickly. "Sir, I need you help." And proceeded to tell him about The Shack. And with that, these two – the President and the student – joined forces and made history. During the meeting, Perk offered to pay the University a cut. Darden accepted. He asked for the old lumber around the site to build The Shack. Darden agreed.

One by one, things fell into place. A construction worker offered to assist in building The Shack, so it would be safe. We got a permit to operate a business on University property, and we ordered a sign that said, Perklum's Place. The "Lum" part came from our new partner's name: Lum Anderson. The Shack eventually became the largest Big Orange Soda account in Charlottesville.

At first, there was a small icebox for drinks ((meaning a block of ice), and sandwiches and Nabs, Moon Pies and Little Debbie Cakes and penny candy.

The wives and husbands – Lum and Janet, Perk and me – made the sandwiches. ALL the sandwiches. And they were fabulously huge, thick sandwiches that sold for 65 cents each. Our egg salad was so rich and wonderful that the sandwiches were three inches tall. We used Kraft mayonnaise, good pickle relish and a whisper of onion and lot of pepper. The egg salad would squirt out all around when you bit into the sandwich and people loved them. They always sold out first!

We made tall bologna sandwiches with lettuce, tomato and a thick slab of cheese with mustard on one side and mayonnaise on the other. I'm talking "slathered." Thick peanut butter and jelly that stuck to the roof of your mouth, and plain bologna sandwiches with good mustard and a ½ inch thick cut of bologna with homemade pickles were popular, too. People loved everything we made!

Our count hit one hundred sandwiches per day. The boys hired two extra students to help and The Shack stayed open at night with sandwiches made to order.

One day Perk came racing into the trailer, "We just put a big, I mean a *big*, cooler in The Shack."

"What did that cost you?" I asked nervously.

"Nothing!" He yipped.

"How come?" I asked.

"You are now looking at the owner of the largest Big Orange drink account in Charlottesville!"

"You swear?" I asked dubiously.

"I swear!" He shouted.

"And they gave you a cooler?" I was floored.

"I swear!"

Suddenly I hollered, "You can't use a cooler, you haven't got any electricity, you nut!"

"I'll get it." He said staunchly.

"You'll get it." I said, in total disbelief. "Ha."

"Watch this." And Perk left the trailer. He entered President Darden's office again and told the secretary that it was an emergency.

"Send him in." President Darden's voice came over the speaker.

"What's the problem Mr. Perkinson? This better be good."

"I need electricity, President Darden. I need it now!"

"In that little shack? That would cost some money, sir. I'm not inclined to do that." Darden spoke firmly.

"I really need it, sir. That shack is now the largest Big Orange drink account in this city. The distributor gave me a cooler..."

"Let me get this straight," Darden interrupted. "We're the biggest account in Charlottesville?"

"Yes, sir," replied Perk. "We are!"

Darden started laughing. "Wait'll I tell my wife!" He stood there, considering the potential. "Let's see now. The University gets a cut of your profits, right?"

"Yes, sir."

"So, the more you make, the more we make?"

"Yes, sir." Perk grinned.

"Okay! So I'll get an electrician right on it." Darden scribbled a note to himself. "We'll need a key to The Shack."

"You've already got one, sir."

"Fine, fine," said Darden. "By the way Mr. Perkinson, how's law school?"

"Law school's good, sir. But I really have to work hard…I mean, being out of school and in the Army for so long…"

"As long as school stays good you're fine." Darden laughed again and shook his head. "The biggest Big Orange account in Charlottesville! Wait until I tell my wife!"

Doing Babies

I had a slight stomach ache. A queasy feeling. A sense of unwell being.

"The flu." I said to myself. It persisted, then began to localize into a time span - mornings.

"A pain in the neck." I said to myself. To myself, not my young husband, because by this time we were feeling totally landlocked in the middle of law school. I tried to let him be a student as much as possible and I tried not to be a problem wife. Things went so much better if the wives were no problem, or sad or sick or anything.

Then it happened. The flu turned out to be a baby on the way. My God, a baby. Oh, I knew how I got it all right, but I didn't. I was operating off the same mentality I had as a little girl of seven.

"Mamma, can I have some of that cold cream?" It was Elizabeth Arden's Orange Blossom skin-nourishing, just-on-the-market new product.

"I guess so." She got up from her dressing table and walked over to me, snubbed down in the her bed.

"We'll put a little here" - on my nose - "and a little here - my face was dots of Orange Blossom - "and then smooth it all over." That was the first time I felt female.

I remember. The rest is crystal clear in my memory too.

"Mamma, where do babies come from?" this, after the light was out and I was snuggled up close to her. Daddy was out of town.

Silence.

"Mamma - are you asleep?"

"No, thinking."

I watched the snow swirling and filling in the gaps of the tree outside.

"You know the Orange Blossom in the face cream?" She asked carefully.

"Um-hmm."

"Well, the Orange Blossom comes from a bud. First, there's the bud - then the blossom - then the fruit. And that's the way a baby does. God puts the bud in your stomach, it blossoms, and you have a baby."

I turned over slowly. "That was it?" Even at seven, I felt let down. I knew, but I didn't.

Still - I liked sharing a secret with my mother.

Us women.

I remember.

Now, I was becoming the "Mamma," and the only thing blossoming around here was my body. It blossomed until I didn't have any faith in it anymore. It's very strange not being able to see your feet! To ensure the baby a bright future, I fell asleep every night saying a rosary for it. And every night, Perk would quietly take the rosary out of my hand and place it on an old-fashioned enormous radio beside our bed that served as a bedside table.

If he had time, he would rub my stomach with Mother's Friend (a lotion to prevent stretch marks). At first, he would carefully fill up my belly button to overflowing and then rub gently to coat all of my slightly bulging stomach. When I got really pregnant my belly button disappeared completely. No dimple, just a small flesh-flower sitting daintily in the middle of this enormous stomach that was as smooth and unmarred as a baby's bottom.

Once the baby began to move, it turned into a hilarious scenario of vigorous baby bumpings and us lovingly pushing the bumps back! The moment the Mother's Friend went on, the bumping and kicks would begin, and we would laugh uncontrollably.

While I was in labor, my young husband tried desperately to study in the waiting room of the University Hospital. His biggest exam was the next day. He wrote at the top of his exam: "Sir, if my handwriting is illegible, please excuse. We had our first baby last night. It's a girl." He passed.

When I opened my eyes, I knew two things: it was over and we had a daughter: Mary Pamela Perkinson. She had a lopsided face and lots of dark hair that stood up on her head like a wheat field. She was decidedly beautiful!

My mother slept quietly in the chair beside my bed, her hand resting on top of mine. Beyond her, coming through the window, was an easy movement of air filled with fragrance. It smelled like acres of orange blossoms. A sense of wonderful well-being swept over me that June morning.

Then I remembered. "Us women" meant us:

My mother.

And me.

And Pam.

The idyllic sense of motherhood that comes with a new baby is an amazing thing in that it quickly dissipates memories of any difficulties with pregnancy. That was not exactly true in my case.

Between the success of The Shack and the later joy of a new baby lay a difficult journey for me. My first pregnancy was tough going.

Barfing my cookies as I smashed out sandwiches for the Shack was not among the high moments of my life. In fact, it moved me to ward a new "consciousness level". Morning after morning took on the same unreality of quiet desperation.

"Perk, pu-lease don't make me do those egg salad sandwiches. I'm so sick..." I'd pull the covers over my head.

"Listen, Thelma, I know you're sick, but you're the one who wanted this baby and I've got studying to do before classes. Now let's see you be a woman about this."

"I'll do those sandwiches if it kills me," I'd fume to myself. I usually managed to finish four or five sandwiches before I had to run for the bathroom. I'd return, fix five more and then holler out, "Oh, God no, not again!"

One morning I managed to finish the sandwiches and get myself dressed in time to catch the bus to the University Student Health Clinic. As I rushed in, I proclaimed, "I've got to see Dr. Ellerson! Now!" Then I promptly threw up in the trash basket.

Seated in Dr. Ellerson's office, I pleaded, "You've got to do something. My life is really awful. I can't stand up sometimes." The tears began to spill. "I can't teach."

Dr. Ellerson handed me a Kleenex. "That bad, huh?"

I looked at him with great angst.

"Okay, okay, let's go to the Emergency Room."

"Now?" I questioned.

"Yep, I'll drive you in my car. It's right out in front. I'll get you a shot for nausea and leave a standard order..."

I shook my head. "You don't want to do that. You can't put me in your car."

"That bad, huh?"

I nodded.

"Okay, you stay here. I'll be back in ten minutes."

In ten minutes he walked back in with a shot from and standing order at the emergency room for more shots, day or night.

"That's wonderful." I said gratefully.

"I can drive over every morning about 5:30 and get a shot." I told him. "That'll really help with the sandwich problem."

"What sandwich problem?"

So I explained about The Shack and the sandwiches. But mostly about the egg salad sandwiches and Perk being upset with me.

He listened quietly and then leaned toward me and said quietly, "That son of a bitch."

My eyes flew open wide. It was so unexpected. I clapped my hand to my mouth, then suddenly I giggled.

He chuckled. "Sorry, but that needed to be said."

The smile faded from my face. "Yes, it did," I said soberly. Then I stepped further into adulthood.

"But I did provoke him." I said sorrowfully. "He does have school."

"Yeah, and he has a wife and a baby on the way. It's your turn, Thelma. Just remember that!" He was becoming quite angry. "I'm getting disgusted by what I see happening. The wives count less and less, and the men are all getting carried away with their own sense of importance."

"Really? Do you really see that?" I asked. "I thought it was just me."

"Thelma, you're too smart for that." He answered impatiently. "I know you're supposed to back up your husbands – and God knows the women here are marvelous, but this clinic is getting overwhelmed by the number of_ wives, not the students, beginning to break down." By now he was striding arround the office.

"I can't believe it's that bad." I said. "I don't hear the wives complain."

"And that's another thing," he interrupted. "The wives are not supposed to complain. You're not supposed to have problems...or to be a problem."

"Sometimes I feel that way, but Perk says I'm emotional and need to grow up."

80

"Hunh," Dr. Ellerson grunted. "Not so".

"So what do I do?"

"Well, seems to me you need to become the head of this family and begin to open up a space for you and the baby. Take less responsibility for your child-husband and more responsibility for your lives, and tell Frank Perkinson what you're doing."

"People will think I'm terrible if I do that." I said. "You know that's not okay on Copeley Hill."

Dr. Ellerson gave a wry smile. "It's more okay than you think. We're putting this idea to every wife who comes in here with fever blisters all over their faces or raging headaches or they can't eat or can't sleep or they hate sex. And they wonder what's wrong with them?!" his voice trailed off.

"Get it straight, Thelma, or you're going to have a sad life. Matter of fact, as good at being students as the men are, as stalwart as the wives are, this whole experiment is going to blow sky high someday."

"What do you mean, sky high?" Now, I was really upset.

"I give it ten years at max!"

"Throughout the whole country?" I asked, incredulously.

He nodded, "For the whole country, for all the married students." Dr. Ellerson was firm.

I was visibly shaken. He was talking divorce? Divorce was a shameful and unacceptable thing in 1949. People did it, but they paid a price. Divorce for me? Never!

"The couples are not going to stay together! They can't, and these marriages aren't really marriages; they are, well, arrangements."

My nausea had subsided and a knot in my stomach had taken its place.

"Arrangements," I repeated after him. "How do you figure that?"

"Okay, here it is: the husband doesn't go to work each day and bring his paycheck home every two weeks. He doesn't stay home in the evenings and on weekends to do things with his wife and family and friends. He doesn't have time to solve problems because he's studying. He can't be upset; he has a test; there can be very few crises; he might fail."

"That's true," I said. "Only I just hadn't thought of it that way."

"Well, that's only the tip of the iceberg." Dr. Ellerson stopped speaking as a knock came on the door and another doctor at the clinic came in.

"How's she doing?" Dr. Wright asked, nodding toward me.

"Well, I've managed to stop her from throwing up all over our clinic," Dr. Ellerson said wryly, "but I think I'm making her sick in another way…"

"Yeah?" Dr. Wright leaned against the doorway.

"Well, I'm lecturing to her about what we see around here, so she can be aware of what's going on Copeley Hill."

"Oh, I'm aware, Dr. Ellerson," I interrupted, "but I just thought it was me and that I was spoiled and needed to 'grow up'." My voice trailed off.

"Damn! There it is again!" Dr. Wright growled to Dr. Ellerson. "Let me tell you something, dear ma'am, (he called all the student's wives that, and we loved it!), we have a healthy respect for the young women of Copeley Hill. They are remarkable. The husbands are getting everything! Everything! They get school free, books free, a little money to live on, a wife takes care of all their needs – cooking, cleaning, washing, and gives them sex and brings home a paycheck. Boy, how can you beat that? I'll tell you. She never, never upsets them."

"But the men work so hard." I interjected.

"Yeah, doing what they dreamed of doing – going to college – doing it in a way that isolates and protects them from the real world." Dr. Ellerson leaned forward. "My God, Thelma, you don't think living with 350 married couples on Copeley Hill is the 'real world' do you?"

"It ain't what I'd choose." I said wryly.

"And," asked Dr. Wright pointedly, "What would you choose?"

"I'd choose a little better food, a little more money and just an inexpensive dress, or shoes or underwear now and then." I stopped, looked at both of them and started to tear up. "But most of all, most of all, I'd be able to go to concerts or the ballet or movies or out to dinner, now and then. I miss those things. I miss joy. I miss friends over to eat a cheap, wonderful meal I've cooked in a cute little apartment I've decorated from the Goodwill."

I paused, thoughtfully, "having been a college student in New York doesn't make this any easier! I never dreamed that the inside of the Copeley Hill would be so drab and boring and unromantic."

"Aha! Now you've got a yardstick for reality! And what we want you to do," nodding toward Dr. Wright, "is talk to Perk about yourself and your dreams and how you feel."

"He's right." Dr. Wright agreed. "You've got time before the baby comes to put new ideas into place. And keep them there! Because, dear ma'am, when a baby comes – as wonderful as they are – they blow dreams into a cocked hat."

Dr. Ellerson growled, "All to HELL is where they get blown!"

I slowly put my head in my hands. "What have I done to myself?" I asked.

"You're living your life." Dr. Ellerson said kindly. "And if you see it with truth, you'll know better what to do and how to live it."

"And fight like the devil for what you believe is right for you and your children." Dr. Wright was adamant. "These men are going to be a handful when they get out of here."

"And yet we honestly feel that they are fine young men basically." Dr. Ellerson added, "that's not it. What we know that most people don't know is these men are more like your sons than your husbands. They come first and they are spoiled in this environment. When you leave, we believe this pattern will follow you. It may diminish, but it will be there."

I grew up a lot in the months that followed. I talked more about my dreams and what I wanted and the things I missed while we were here living on Copeley Hill. In essence, I developed a philosophy – a young philosophy, granted – for myself and my family. And I began to take back some of myself. A philosophy surely ahead of its time.

A few years later Betty Frieden came roaring out of McCalls Magazine her first women's lib article. As Mo would say, "That sure blew their skirts up!"

Dr. Ellerson was right. Within five years the divorces began and during the next five years, the divorce rate for married students soared all over the country.

I realized the lessons I was learning would move me toward the wisdom and maturity I needed to have.

One particular incident stands out in my memory. It involved Bobby and Ethyl Kennedy. Perk saw Bobby Kennedy frequently at the Law School. Sunday Mass was the only place I ever saw the Kennedys; Ethyl Skakell and Bobby. They always sat on the first pew and exuded an aura that read well-situated; well-connected and well-fed.

God, forgive me, I envied them, and often had a difficult time concentrating on the Mass because I was so busy concentrating on them. The thing that struck me the most (even at 21) was the projected attitude which clearly said they were golden people, sophisticated and above the fray.

In our situation, the Kennedys stood out, and were of course, envied. The Kennedys didn't mix with the law group, and they didn't show up for law school dances. Their seemingly seamless life flowed on, evenly, and ours bumped and lurched toward the same ever mutual goal, a law degree.

On a chill November Sunday, Ethyl Skakell arrived at Mass in a maternity outfit. She was pregnant with her first baby.

On the same chill November Sunday I arrived at Mass in a maternity outfit. I was pregnant with my first baby.

I saw Ethyl, but I don't think she saw me.

The following week, our crowd had gathered at the Sims' apartment for some serious partying. I mentioned the Kennedys. The snorting and hooting that came from several of the men set me back.

"Good God," Johnny Sims said, "he's on the Law Review with us! I can't tell you what an arrogant S.O.B. he is...and mouth! He's got the foulest mouth at the University!"

The other men nodded vigorously.

"Absolutely!"

"A garbage pail," Fletch Watson added.

"Hunh," Frank Parlier spoke up. "Don't tell me! I was part of the Committee to the Dean to get him kicked off the Law Review!"

"I don't believe you," I said. "I'm in the midst of men who landed on Normandy. Kip, over there, was sunk on the Indianapolis, and you," I turned to Frank Watkins -- "were wounded on Iwo Jima. You guys are complaining about swearing?"

"You got it," Frank replied. "Swearing in the Army is one thing, but you don't hear us swearing now...not in front of women and not at the Law School!"

"That's true," Marge Boozer nodded. "I'm amazed."

"So you made a conscious effort to remove Robert Kennedy from the _Law Review_?" I asked.

"We all did."

"How come?"

Frank propped his permanently stiff leg on the coffee table. "We, my dear, are Virginia gentlemen! The school expects us to respect the Honor Code, wear a coat and tie to all classes, and hold our liquor well.

"And?" asked Mo.

"We sat down when we got there. We told him we had a problem with Kennedy. We said it had to stop. Either Kennedy had to go or we would."

"Man, oh, man," breathed May Francis. "Tell us exactly ... word for word..." she insisted.

"OK. The Dean listened until we finished and said, "This is a very serious accusation, but I can't believe it's as bad as you say. Maybe he goes too far in cussing or something like that...but to put him off the <u>Law Review</u>? ...I don't think so. 'Besides' the Dean says, 'ya'll are big boys. You've probably heard a lot worse that that;' and he's got this stupid, jackass smirk on his face."

Fletch interrupted. "That was a big mistake, I can tell you. All of us got mad at the same time, but it was Frank Watkins who blew the hole in the roof!" Fletch grinned.

"Frank stood up on the lame leg of his, limped over to the Dean's desk and got right in his face. 'Well, SIR, seems we've got to initiate you into the Kennedy Club. And I'm telling you straight, when we leave here, we're going to Darden and tell him the same thing! And another thing. Don't patronize us. We don't like it...I don't like it...I'm no college kid.'

"Dear God in heaven," I said, shaking my head in disbelief.

"That's nothing," said Parlier, "there was a lot more. By the time we finished, the Dean was furious with Kennedy. 'That's not what this school is about and that behavior is trash'."

"Yeah, he did say that" agreed Fletch, "but I loved it when Frank answered back 'the man is absolute pig trash and -- if what he says his father has taught him is true--besides hiring prostitutes for all his sons--the father is pig trash, too!'"

"Oh, my God" exclaimed Mo. "What happened?"

"The Dean sat there like he was frozen," said Parlier. "Then he reached over, flicked on his intercom and told his secretary to make an appointment with Darden immediately."

"Was Kennedy put off the *Law Review*?" I asked.

"Hell, no!" exploded Johnny Sims. "Daddy has donated too much money to the school." He turned to Fletch. "Remember someone was telling us when his brother Jack was here he had an incomplete in some class and even though he was supposed to graduate, the professor wouldn't pass him. He had an incomplete and that was that. There was a God-awful row, and somehow Jack graduated. Poppa's money..."

"I'll tell you what did happen," Parlier snorted. "That S.O.B. has never uttered a foul word around any of us since. Never! Ever!"

By now, we were applauding and whistling.

"Somebody rode his arse to the barn, I can tell you! And I tell you something else, nobody would have handled it the way Frank Watkins did. With that peg leg and balding head and roaring voice. That Dean knew he would beat the beejeesus out of Kennedy if it didn't stop." Parlier said.

"And...and," he continued, "that Dean of the Law School of the UVA, a good man, I might add, learned a new lesson in deanmanship."

By now Parlier was the total clown, lisping slightly as a result of too many Purple Passions.

"He learned not to be a stuffed-shirt jackass and pompous idiot with the law students' cause we's Men!" With that Parlier made a flying leap for the sofa and landed across the laps of its occupants.

For a second, there was silent disbelief; and then laughter filled the trailer. Frank Parlier, the French exchange student who took part in the French Resistance, son of a French cabinet minister and a beautiful American mother, our proper and polished member of our crowd had lost his proper.

We all looked at each other. "Do you believe it?"

"I never thought I'd ever see the day!"

The months went by, the Masses went by, and I continued to sit behind "The Royal Presence"! If I had just been able to sit in a pew in front of Ethyl and Bobby it would have been simple, but they had the front pew.

Then, the-lesson-to-be-learned began to surface. As I became larger and larger and Ethyl became larger and larger I saw this couple move farther apart in their pew. There were no brief glances between them. I never saw hm offer her a helping hand toward her when she tried to stand--especially that last month. Nothing. The imagined levels of equality disappeared, and I saw what I was supposed to learn: money didn't stop the backaches; money didn't put out the steadying hand, and money didn't prevent our bodies from bulging. We were both the same. So maybe Ethyl would need money to smooth over a life that might be really scruffy if she didn't have it. (The rumors were that they were members of the Farmington Country Club and that Ethyl never cooked, or cleaned or...)

I knew in an instant that I would never live scruffy, that would not be me, whether I had money or not. I might struggle, I might be fearful, but I damn well would not be scruffy.

I, Thelma Crosby Perkinson, walked into Mass one fine June day carrying my new baby, Pam.

She, Ethyl Skakell Kennedy, walked into Mass on the same fine day carrying her new baby, Katherine.

Standing behind her I felt relieved to see that her baby was obviously healthy and she was fine. My affection for her surprised me.

As we left church, I smiled at the Kennedys and said "Congratulations. I love your baby."

Ethyl and Bobby smiled weakly and passed on.

"Yep," I said to myself. "They need that money!"

Just then a woman moving down the aisle next to Perk and me looked over and smiled.

"Congratulations! I love your baby."

We smiled back. "Thank you. We do, too!"

Coming of Age

The income from my music studio wasn't dependable. I had to get a job. Three couldn't live on $75.00 a month. I called Personnel. "I hear you have an opening coming up in the Housing Office."

"Yes, in about six weeks or so." She said.

"Well, I'm a student's wife and I'm interested. (Student's wives got preference.) What do I have to do?"

"Okay, you have to pass a typing and shorthand test." The voice on the other end of the line said. "It pays $168.00 a month."

Oh, God, I thought, I'm dead. I can't type or take shorthand. I can type a little...but shorthand?

Fierce resolution filled my bosom. "I've got about four weeks," I said to myself "to learn typing and shorthand. I'll teach myself!"

I rented a typewriter and bought some shorthand tablets. I did nothing but tend the baby and work on the skills. The typing began to smooth out, and I increased my speed. Each evening, I'd grab someone from a nearby trailer to correct my typing and clock my shorthand speed. Day by day, it got faster and more accurate, but my goal of fifty words a minute eluded me.

As for the shorthand, I made up my own version based on a shorthand called "Pittman." My father taught me the basics just for fun and would play games giving me dictation. If a word had an 'ing' ending, you'd write the word then put a long dash; if it ended in 'ed', you'd write the word and put a short dash.

It made sense to me to put down "depend- -" for "dependable." 'A', and 'the' were "/." And so on.

Little had I realized, that years later I'd reach back to my childhood games for something so important. During the day I'd try to take down my new shorthand from the radio. It was crazy because I never could go back to check the content. But I kept on. "I'll do this," I'd tell myself between diapers and feedings, burpings and exhaustion. I was feeling more than a little abandoned.

Perk had literally vacated the trailer because he couldn't sleep and he couldn't study and the new baby was a complete shock to our previous quiet life. After three years of living completely for the student in the family, we needed to focus on other things. He found my nursing the baby "unsettling..." It reminded him of European peasants. I found him to be a complete idiot and wondered what manner of man I'd married. What else was hidden in the darker side of Perk?

Once my mother heard I was having trouble nursing, she started to sail into Charlottesville with a more than ample supply of beer every few days. One day she met up with Perk. "This is for Thelma," she said. Then just as quickly as she'd come, she sailed away.

"The beer," she said in her wickedly sweet way, "is an old-fashioned remedy to give the mother plenty of milk."

As she left one day, she said, "that precious baby looks just like her daddy!" The she gave him a hug and winked at me over his shoulder. He stood there at the doorway, waving good-bye, not realizing she was furious. My mother was a real lady. She never showed her disappointment in Perk.

I told my girlfriends on the Hill, "Look, I can't do this alone. That husband of mine has freaked out with this baby." The women nodded knowingly. "I need help every night for about an hour of dictation.

"So what's the problem? We'll take turns dictating."

"Seven days a week?" I asked incredulously.

"You are now officially booked seven days a week." They said.

I have to say, quite frankly, there was a great amount of snickering by my girlfriends at my homemade shorthand, mixed with a lack of belief in my faulty transcribing. They teased but they helped. Like the typing, the shorthand slowly took form. My typing developed a steady rhythmic speed and the dictation transcribed with more and more accuracy.

The month was up and I was ready. My girlfriends were terrific.

"Don't worry, I'll take Pam," said a stay-at-home mother. "Take time dressing and don't get nervous."

"Stay calm." This advice came from my friend who worked as a secretary. "Don't type as fast as you can. Hold back just a little, you'll do better."

"That's the damnedest stenography routine I've ever seen, but I think you just might get that job," said Mo.

The Personnel Office was waiting for me. "Go in there," said a kind, young woman, "and type this two page letter for us."

I sat myself straight in the chair, made sure my paper was set straight in the typewriter and began. The typing went well in spite of my shaking hands.

"That wasn't too bad," I said, encouraging myself.

The young woman stuck her head in the room, "Are you okay?" she asked.

I nodded.

"Okay, come over here beside me." She pulled out a chair for me. "I want to give you dictation."

"I'm not going to make it. I'm going to lose this wonderful job. Oh, God...I really need your help!" I said to myself.

And so, we began. Her voice was evenly paced and calm as she spoke. My writing was just the opposite: it lurched and slashed and dashed seemingly all over the page. Time was interminable. Then I was done!

She looked at my shorthand tablet for a long moment, then up into my eyes.

"Can you transcribe this on the typewriter?" She tried to hide her doubt.

I nodded and picked up my tablet and walked into the other room. As I began to type, I felt calmer and calmer. I could read this stuff! I was transcribing perfectly and typing well.

I passed the test and I got the job. Many months later after they knew me, the girls in Personnel told me they were amazed and they had all made bets on who would pass the tests and who wouldn't.

Laughingly, they said, "Nobody would bet on you! You were so white with your hands trembling...you were a sight! And then we saw that shorthand!

"Are you speaking of my super-duper Pittman?" I asked coyly.

"Is that what it's called?"

"I've never seen anything like it," one said. "Where in the name of God did you learn it?"

"From my dad. That's the shorthand they used in the early 1900's and 1920's. We played games with it."

"You were so nervous and I felt so bad for you," my dictator at the Personnel office stated. "What was going on?"

"You mean, besides needing that job desperately?" I though a moment. "I've just had my first baby. That leaves you shaky..." All the women nodded knowingly. "And I have come to the realization I have another baby on my hands. My husband. That left me deeply shaken."

"Yes, that can." The older Personnel girl agreed. "And you know what? This happens more often than you think."

"Well," I brightened. "I got the job, I love the job, and I have the greatest baby-sitter in the world -- a girl who is wonderful named Josephine , so I'm as happy as can be. I teach music at night and bring in every dime I can and I am proud of myself." I grinned in a cocky manner.

"Well, after seeing you take that dictation," my Personnel mentor said, "and then haul off and transcribe it, you're my one hero!" She paused. "Seriously, you've got guts, girl."

I sat there smiling.   ——

Cleaning Day
Marge, Thel, Mo'

Party at the Pattersons
Bob and Anne

Veterans of Normandy, The Battle of the Bulge, Italy, France, South Pacific and Iwo Jima

Graduation

The Old Man of Iwo

Frank Watkins was the old man of the Law School. He was around thirty and though we never told, he looked older. He had a rugged face - a great face - but rugged - a receding hairline, a stocky body and a stiff right leg he got on Iwo Jima.

"What happened to yer leg?" people would ask.

"Got it and -- AND a ma-dal on "Iwo,' he'd reply, dragging on his pipe.

"Whatsa madal?"

"A madal is a madal, you fool!" They pin it on your uniform," he'd laugh.

"Oh, a MEDAL."

"Yeah, a madal." Frank would say through clenched teeth - under his breath he'd add, "you son-of-a-bitch."

It was really none of their damn business. He was sick and tired of being asked and even more sick and tired of the leg he knew would never bend again.

Other than that, things were not too tough on ole Frank. He had a generous disability check, he had the GI Bill and Copeley Hill had given him and his wife, Hawk a double apartment in the barracks apartments for them and their three children.

They proceeded to decorate by tearing down walls, adding mahogany paneling and book shelves everywhere, Early American furniture Hawk found and refinished plus rugs and draperies. The whole nine yards. They didn't spend a lot because they were clever at adding good taste and hard work to their pennies.

They ended up with four bedrooms, a large bath, living room, dining room, big kitchen, and a study for Frank. It was charming.

Since he attended his full seven years of school - four of pre-Law, three of Law - at U.VA. It made sense to create a comfortable home if you could.

Generally, the couples on Copeley were as likeable as Frank and Hawk and most tried to be kind and tolerant. Certainly that was the case in our group. Except for one jarring note: one of the wives.

She was smart and capable and had a great job. She was ultra-conservative and would brook no nonsense.

Fortunately she had some sense of humor, but she was hypercritical of anything or anyone who was offbeat or colorful or individualistic.

She was a rather plain young woman who lived in a plain trailer, dressed in a plain way, played bridge three times a week and lo-o-o-oved Copeley Hill.

She mentally compartmentalized people who didn't meet her standards; and ever so often would jab another criticism into some poor soul's niche.

I always felt my niche was full to overflowing and had been for many months.

"Who gave her permission to walk on water?" was asked from time to time. "Why does she have to be so judgmental."

"I don't know." I'd shake my head. "If she likes you, you're safe; but if she doesn't, she is unrelenting with small barbs and attitudes. It makes me want to shake her!

"Besides, I find her boring and colorless and hurtful," I stated flatly.

"Have you told Perk?" a neighbor asked.

"Who, me?" I yipped. "Never! I'm not going to open my mouth. This will all be over, one day, and I won't have to see her again. I also know she never shows this side to Perk; but then, she likes the men so he wouldn't be aware of what was going on."

It was hard, but right up to the day we graduated, she never knew my feelings. I was proud of that. Of all the couples, Frank and Hawk Watkins were my favorite.

He was unflappable and easy, and a country boy. The mark of "country lawyer" was already on him in the quiet, intelligent way he spoke and in his simplicity. What he was _not_, was "a good ole boy".

Frank was just the opposite. My favorite thing about him was his hidden sophistication and ability to mix with all kinds.

Eenie Nash, one of the first women to be admitted to the Law School was a buddy of his. She was smart and moneyed and had poodle parties several times a year at her parent's estate.

Poodle parties were attended by the upper crust around Charlottesville who would bring their poodles and pedigreed dogs for a Sunday soiree.

Hawk called one day to chat and said, "Guess where we're going next Sunday?"

"Where?"

"To Eenie's to a party for people and their la-dee-dah dogs!"

"Get out of here!"

"Swear to God, I just got the invitation. And you haven't heard it all. Frank's taking Sheriff."

"That old hound dawg of ya'll's?" I doubled over with laughter. "Hawk, you've got to stop him!"

"There's no stopping him. You know Frank when he gets his heart set on something!"

Needless to say, the story spread over the Hill in short order and then, the Law School. But somehow, it didn't get back to Eenie.

The Poodle Party – Sunday arrived, and a small crowd gathered down by the barrack-apartments to witness the "setting forth." Out came Frank and Hawk looking like a million bucks; and out came that good ole over-weight, low-slung Basset hound, Sheriff, on a big ole frayed rope tied to his collar.

We stood there in disbelief for a second and then, starting laughing. You could have heard us all over the Hill.

Later, we heard that Frank entered the party first with Sheriff; Eenie almost fainted, then slowly got a huge grin on her face. The various and sundry guests stood frozen, took a big swig of their drink, then tried to nod civilly.

After a time it became clear all the dogs liked Sheriff; it was clear Eenie liked Sheriff; so what the Hell!..everybody else decided they liked Sheriff, too!

Besides, as disarming as Frank and Hawk were, who could resist them and their obvious wit? So they became regular expected guests at Eenie's Poodle Parties until Frank graduated and they left for a small, Virginia City to practice law.

Hawk was a fine friend and a marvelous mother. And probably the greatest cook I ever knew. She cooked French, she cooked Italian, she cooked country Southern that would beat the greatest chefs of the Fiefdom.

She was of average looks and was a large-bone of a girl from the country who had never had an opportunity to go to college, because of the Great Depression which left many families in America living from hand to mouth.

I never forgot her telling me, one day setting on my steps, that she had asked Frank. "How are your going to feel about having a wife who is not educated? You're so far above me, I'm afraid you'll be embarrassed. Tears stung my eyes. "What did he say?" I asked.

"He said 'I chose you because I was proud of you and I plan to be proud of you until I die, Hawk. I can't imagine life without you.'"

Hawk put her head down on her knees for along moment. "Isn't he wonderful?"

"Both of you are," I said. "And I can't imagine our lives without you." And I hugged her.

Sometime later, Frank's leg began to swell and hurt and give the doctors grave concern. There was a real possibility he could lose it if the problem wasn't brought under control. The situation went on for months; and finally, Hawk called the crowd to come for drinks and dinner, and drinks and dessert, and drinks.

"Frank needs to cut loose. So let's do it! But I'm warning everybody I think he's planning to really tie one on. Brace yourselves..." she laughed.

And that's just what happened. The company was wonderful, the food was wonderful, the drinks were consumed with abandon and it turned into the wildest party we'd ever put on: singing, dancing, joke-telling all at the top of our voices...but not Frank.

His mood had slowly turned downward and he began to talk about his leg and about the War. We'd never heard him to that before. Hawk tried to distract him, but there was not turning the torrent aside. The avalanche was clearly coming, and we simply settled ourselves on the floor, or in laps, or in chairs and waited.

"Ya know, after I'd fought all the way up the damn booy of Italy I got winged on my head trying to help three ga-zillion soldiers take Monte Casino. That Monastery, sitting on top of a sheared-off mountain, had dead men and dead parts hanging everywhere; and Germans right on the top, shooting down the cliffs. I saw a lot of blasted faces.

"Hell," I thought, "nothing could get worse. I'd done part of Europe; I'd done half of Italy and still had the other half to go...when we were ordered to the South Pacific. Jesus, the South Pacific!"

"You never told us!" Perk interrupted. "Where were you?"

"And I'm not gonna. I'll spare you the boring gory details and take you right to the Big One." Frank held up his glass for Hawk to refill.

"Which one was the Big One?"

"I-WO," Frank stated. "I-WO JI-MA, my little man. Iwo Jima..." he said, solemnly. "...and when I really die, it will be easy. I died a million times on Iwo."

We sat very still. We waited, braced for what was coming.

"Our landing craft had its landing moat blasted off just as we were lowering it. I was knocked out and back into the boat everybody was on shore and I grabbed my gear and head out, too."

"It was a slaughter. The water was bright red and you couldn't see the bottom. I kept screaming for my best buddy, Robert, and plowing past the beach up into the jungle's edge, looking for him. I knew I needed to find him.

"I came to this clearing and this God-damn Jap had his gun aimed at Robert's genitals and right then, the Gook fired. Another Jap ran up and sprayed Robert with his flame-thrower, yelling Japanese and laughing.

"They never saw me until too late. I cut them down with my machine gun! By now Robert had stopped screaming. He was dead...but the Japs weren't. I walked over slowly, picked up the flamethrower and burned their PECKERS OFF!!

We were too frozen to show horror...not a word...not a movement Hawk was the same.

Frank looked around at us silently "And you know what? I've never regretted making them feel what my buddy felt. Never! And you know what? Just as I was leaning over to pull Robert's dog tags off, one of those son-of-bitches shot me in the leg and then died. Damn good thing he did."

He sat back, exhausted.

"I gotta go to bed," he stated, unsteadily. Fletch and Johnny Sims stood up, got him on his feet and headed toward the bedroom.

For several days after the dinner party, Frank had to stay in bed. He was very, very ill; he cried frequently and his leg was worse. He shook a lot, and would break out in heavy sweats. So much so, Hawk changed the bed three and four times a day.

We would stop by and quietly inquire from Hawk about the unusual situation. Frank had never been known to do anything such as this. Ever. The doctors were kept informed morning and night by Hawk.

Then, one bright, crisp, October morn, Frank Watkins appeared at the Law School looking like a new man. His leg had almost healed and his limp was different...a small limp, not a big rolling limp.

"What happened?" I asked Hawk.

She smiled a huge smile. "The doctors said our dinner party was the turning point. He finally felt safe with friends he knew loved him. That night was the anniversary of Robert's death. Do you believe it? ...And he got smashed enough that all that he'd been holding in for years came pouring out."

"You didn't know this story?" I asked, incredulously.

"Never. Not one word. My God, do you believe what some of these boys have been through?"

I shook my head. "No."

"Where was your Perk?" she asked.

"He wasn't in the War, itself. He was in Italy with the Army of Occupation guarding the trains and riding them all over Italy." I answered.

"So..." I said slowly.

"So..." she said slowly. "We're lucky."

"Yes, we are. And you know what else?" I said. "I really am crazy about being American!"

"Interesting," Hawk answered, "Frank says that all the time."

Stompin' At The Savoy

A group of wives had gathered on the steps of our trailer, one evening, to talk about my red door.

"I can't believe they took your husband to President Darden," Marge Boozer, my new neighbor across the road said. She shook her red hair in disbelief. "Why did they do that?"

I giggled. "Surely you jest!" "That was to show the women of Copeley Hill that they better keep their place or..." I drew a deep breath, "..or their husbands would be punished."

"I can't believe the Mayor would go such lengths," sighed another neighbor, Jenny Crockett.

"Believe it," Hawk Watkins interrupted. "Let me make you aware of how deep this goes. In the past, no women were tolerated in a classroom. If one did come in, the students would start stomping their feet!"

"What?" yelled Marge.

"Yep, that's what would happen," Hawk calmly stated.

"Well," I said slowly, "this is very unsettling. What else is going to happen at Mr. Jefferson's academy of male superiority?"

"Wait'll you go to wives' orientation. Among other things, you'll be told, subtly, how to drink. You either hold your liquor like a Virginia gentleman or you don't drink."

Just then, Beth Anson, the oldest wife on the Hill married to the oldest student on the Hill (thirty-two) walked up "Hey, Miz Perkins, I hear you raised a ruckus over some silly ole door." She grinned wickedly.

"I know, and I'm a little embarrassed," I answered.

"Don't be," she said. "Everybody loved it."

"We were telling Thelma about the foot stomping routine," Marge laughed.

Beth looked amused. "We've been residents of Copeley Hill since it opened and I can tell you that stuff stopped shortly after I got here."

"Really? I wonder why?" I asked.

"Well," Beth said wryly, "here's the story. One day, I had to take a school paper to Bob, my husband. I knew his schedule, so I went to his class during break." She drew a breath. " I walked in, headed toward him, and they started stomping their feet."

"Oh, my God," breathed Hawk, "what did you do?"

"I was horrified! I threw that paper at Bob and practically ran out of that room. But then, I stopped, getting madder and madder!" Beth took a moment to smile. "You know what I did? I turned around and walked back in. I stood with my hands on my hips. How dare those jackasses stomp at me. Here I was in the WAFS for three years flying planes all over god-knows-where in this world, I come out with a letter of merit. No G.I. Bill because we weren't REGULAR SERVICE...and I GET STOMPED AT?" By now Beth's voice was getting louder. "They needed a lesson and I was the woman to teach it to them."

"I started stomping up and down, hard, around the professor's desk, over to the door and back! Bob almost had a stroke!"

"Just then, the professor came in. 'Good morning' I said really loud, and stomped out the door, down the hall and all the way out to the curb!" She took a long breath, "I raised HELL without saying a word!"

The group looked at each other with bugged eyes. Their mouths dropped open and they began to laugh, then scream in total hysterics.

"Ha--a-a"

"Ha-ha-ha, I'm dying!"

"Oh-h-h my stomach!"

By that time near-by citizens of the Hill were gathering and demanding to know the reason for such rowdy behavior. It wasn't long before they were dissolved in laughter. Naturally, the story spread over the Hill and then throughout the school and faculty. Later that week, according to Beth's story, Bill Anson hit an unexpected moment of truth in his life.

"You" said Beth adamantly, "have a battle to wage. The stomping has to stop. Now! It begins with you, then your professor, the dean and the President."

"Aw, Beth, I know it was upsetting, but can't you just let it go? This place is so goofy about its male image I don't know how the students and my professors will take it."

Beth gazed at him in disbelief. "Then I'll go," she was practically shouting, "and tell them who I am...I am a World War II pilot who is damn brave and smart and married to a gutless wonder, who is connected to his "brothers" by one thing...A PENIS!"

"Beth, Beth," Bill tried to say. "You need to calm down."

Beth turned on him, "Don't you dare dismiss my feelings. I don't need to calm down and don't you patronize me, you jackass!" She narrowed her eyes "What's it going to be?"

Bill looked at her narrowly, "I can't decide just like that."

"What's it going to BE?"

"I have to think about it, Beth."

"One, two, th..."

"Ok, Ok" Bill put his hand over his eyes trying to gauge what had just hit him.

"Ok, what? I'm telling you, Bill, if I leave, I'll never come back to this burg or you!"

"I'll go, Beth! I'll go."

"This week!"

"Yes!"

Beth sat down on the sofa, swung her leg back and forth sharply, and looked hard at her husband. Then, she stood up. "That's settled then," she said. "I'm going to the grocery store."

Fortunately for old Bill a notice from the President was posted on all bulletin boards the following Monday:

The rude custom of stomping is now forbidden. All ladies are to be respected

on these grounds by every one of us. If she is not, you will be dismissed from this institution immediately.

A young lady who has served this country brilliantly and bravely, who ferried over twenty-two planes across the Atlantic to our pilots in England, was stomped while looking for her husband in a Law School a classroom last week.

That entire class will be severely reprimanded.

Virginia gentleman?

There is grave question in my mind.

Colgate Darden

The President"

Gimme That Ole Time Religion

It seemed to me the days of Copeley Hill were rather barren of religion and spirituality. Sundays were for "sleeping in" for three-fourths of the dwellers; and religion was rarely discussed until an ex-monastery student, Louis Podesta joined the ranks of the law school.

Then all hell broke loose because he insisted on mocking the monastery, mocking the priest, mocking celibacy rules and mocking Catholics in general...to anyone who'd listen.

Perk's buddies decided there might be a hilarious evening of fireworks (so to speak) if Louis met the Catholic of the crowd. Me. So, invitations were extended and accepted; and neither of us was warned about the other. I had no reason to find him anything but attractive and extremely humorous and quick. That is, until the crowd casually mentioned I was Catholic.

The son-of-a-bitch changed from benign into malevolent in an instant...so fast it made my heart jump. "Oh, My God" he moaned "don't tell me you eat fish on Fridays and go to Mass every Sunday!"

"I do" I replied quietly. I wasn't going to get pulled into it.

"And say your rosary like a good girl," he said, mockingly.

"I do."

"It's a bunch of crap," he said in a raging voice. "How many times in the damn monastery saying the same prayers, the same Latin prayers over and over and thinking about nothin' but women, whispering to each other about women, and all the time acting like we were downright holy while all the time we were nothin' but healthy!"

He caught his breath and squared off again "This *infallibility of the Pope* thing is phony, too. The whole religion is set up as the only religion and the Catholic Church preaches the only real truth!"

Everyone was silent. I sat for a long moment looking straight at him "You got kicked out of the seminary, didn't you? You didn't leave, you got kicked out. That's what all of this is about. You idiot! Don't you come into a group of people you don't know and tune up. At least, not around me! I find you rude, crude, and unattractive and I don't want to ever be around you again."

"Well you didn't invite me here," he began.

"You're cotton pickin' right I didn't but I'm inviting you to leave. You either leave or I will...and...and another thing: if you take my religion away...my faith...what are you going to give me in the place of it?" I spat out.

He sat there looking sullen.

"I thought so. Nothing" "That's what you've got to give me...<u>nothing</u>." I stood up. "I'm leaving."

I turned to the group and said in a measured tone, "Don't ever do this again. It's rotten, not funny." And I left. We didn't speak of religion again until many months later.

In the meantime, Perk never wavered from his struggle to get through law school. He was not a brilliant student. His intellect was adequate but flashes of creativity, deep insight and a quick grasp of the abstract were not his to claim. He made up for some of that by studying--always—with his dictionary open and by plowing and plodding through reams of legal jargon in a steady, slow pace.

As a result, his grades were average but solid. Not good enough to get him on the <u>Law Review</u> to be know as a promising law student, but solid.

The second summer of law school was approaching, and so was the opportunity to take the Bar Exam. Most second-year students took it but never expected to pass it. They simply took it to get the feel of the God-awful experience before trying again in their third year. This first time wasn't life or death; the next time was. They could not practice law until they passed.

So, the men signed up for the month-long seminar that cost $100.00! The men spent six hours each day in the seminar and then until one or two o'clock in the morning studying.

Before long, the wives noticed small irregularities in the husbands' attitudes. Then came the weight loss and nervousness and a pallor from lack of sun.

Wisely, the wives began to plan blanket parties on Saturday nights, no matter what.

"We gotta study" the husbands would whine.

"You've got a wife," we'd snap back. "You're not doing this seven days a week. Absolutely not! This is crazy, and it's making you crazy!"

Reluctantly, they'd give in. Then, they'd proceed to eat and drink everything in sight and become so rowdy we'd have to explain the Bar Exam Syndrome to all our neighbors and apologize profusely. Same thing, every week.

The dreaded day of days arrived and I began to pray like I'd never prayed before except when I was expecting Pam.

My intention was to make a powerful Novena to St. Jude, the help of the hopeless--or was it the hope of the helpless? The Novena is made every hour for six hours; and, according to Catholic beliefs, it is a very powerful Novena, not to be pursued lightly.

I began my earnest petition for my young husband: that he would pass the exam and achieve the admiration of his classmates and professors; so that he would never have to go through this harrowing experience again; so that he would indeed know, by God, he was a lawyer!

The weeks passed, and school began, and more weeks passed, and nothing was heard regarding the Bar Exam.

One morning, while at my job in the University Housing Office, I got a call from Mary Francis Sims.

"Are you sitting down? Have you seen the paper?" she questioned.

"Yes to the first; no to the second."

"Thelma, Perk passed the Bar Exam!"

"What?" I was frozen.

"Perk's passed the Bar Exam!"

"Honest? Honest?" the tears began to slide down my face.

"Listen to this: 'The number of law students statewide to take the Exam was 366 and the number that passed, statewide, was 65!' That's what the newspaper says."

"And Perk was one of the sixty-five?"

"Yep."

"That's incredible! Did Johnny pass?"

"Un-unh."

"I'm sorry, Mary Francis. How about Fletch or the Franks?"

"No one passed in the crowd, and a lot of third-year students didn't pass! They are saying this Bar Exam was absolutely unrealistic if only 65 students out of 366 passed."

"Whew! That's not many at all!" I agreed.

Our friends decided this incredible turn of events must be celebrated...but not with a blanket party. They were taking the Perkinsons out to dinner at the elegant Ivy Inn to show admiration and pride in "one of their own".

I had just come across a new "piss-elegant" recipe that was expensive and glamorous and not the UVA genré. I decided we'd serve these newly discovered French 75's before going to dine. Little did I know that two or three of these would do real damage to the equilibrium! Served in a large champagne glass, the combination of one ounce of gin, one-fourth ounce of Roses' sweetened lime juice and the glass filled to the brim with chilled, dry champagne seemed harmless and delicious! And so we drank one batch, and then another; then, we drank a third batch and ran out of champagne. It was a blessing. By the time we got to the Inn, our words slurred slightly, we missed a step or two, and Parlier began to lisp.

The maitre'd smoothly guided us past the table set for us into a beautiful, small dining room set apart in the back of the Inn. He knew trouble when he saw trouble.

We wined and dined and began to feel as if we didn't have a care in the world. We all were absolutely outstanding "Virginia gentlemen", and acknowledged that fact to each other more than once during the evening.

Frank Watkins stood and drank a toast to Perk and congratulated him on achieving such an accomplishment all on his own.

Perk slowly pushed his chair back and stood with an uncertain expression on his face.

"I've been debating whether to tell you guys something because I'll never hear the end of this, I know; but if I don't tell you, I'm afraid God or Thelma--or maybe both--will strike me dead!"

I sat there looking up at him with a small grin.

"She made a Novena to St. Jude for me to pass the Bar!"

A shout of laughter filled the small room.

"You gotta be kiddin'" yelled Johnny Sims.

"You haven't heard it all" Perk laughed. "St. Jude's the help of the hopeless--"

Here he was interrupted by the belly laughs of his slightly tipsy and doubled over friends.

"Now I'll never know if I did this or St. Jude did this. I gotta admit it, but what the Hell...maybe I did!" He looked around, laughing.

"But get it straight, you pathetic wretches, I'm the one who can practice law right now. Watch your tone of voice to me; and you might try 'Sir' once in a while."

"Yeah! Ha!"

"Right Perkinson," they said sarcastically.

"And," Perk turned toward me, "how about a hand for the praying mantis!" With that, he led a chorus of whistles and applause.

I grinned. "You owe me a diamond watch, someday, when you're rich."

We sat for a few minutes quietly sipping coffee. Then, Fletch spoke up with a surprising statement, "I've been sitting here, watching, and saying to myself 'What a splendid evening this is. I suspect we'll all have money and splendid evenings in the future, but none better than this."

"Fletcher," said Jane surprised, "What a terrific way to end the evening." She hugged him.

The entire senior class and the professors of the law school were fully aware that Perk had passed the Bar, while some of the top students had not. That was acknowledged, generously and then, forgotten. Perk still studied with his dictionary beside him and still made average grades. His job still remained to graduate from law school.

That last year whirled by and suddenly without my realizing it, the time rolled around again for Bar Exams to be taken. The whole, odious journey had to be endured once more by our friends. Four weeks of eighteen-hour days saturated in law, anxiety, and a desperate need to pass the Bar Exam so they could get their license from the state to actually practice law.

It upset Perk and me just to watch from the sidelines.

The evening before the Bar Exam was to be taken, there was a knock at our trailer door.

Perk opened it and saw eight faces peering up at him from the bottom of the steps. "Where's Thelma?" They asked.

He turned and said "I think this is for you" in a knowing way. He stepped aside.

"Hey, ya'll!" I said.

They stood for a moment, and then pushed Fletch Watson forward. "Hey, Miz Praying Mantis, Miz Thelma Lou Perkins. We decided to ask you if you would do that Novena to St. Jude...for us."

"You did?"

"Yes." They nodded. Perk put his arm around me. "For you, she'll do it," he said confidently.

Slowly, I got a devilish look on my face. "Remember the defrocked devil you set loose on me?"

They looked a little sheepish.

"That's three...three" holding my fingers. "masses you guys have to go to with us."

"What?" they yelled.

"You heard me, Pie Face," I said, leaning down into their faces, "and you're to each put one dollar in the plate each Mass."

"What?" They yelled.

"There's more!" I said, evilly, "You're to kneel down right now, raise your right hand and say after me, "I promise I will never bait a Catholic again."

"Aw, come on, Thelma."

"Do it!" I commanded, "Or else I'm not praying."

They hesitated, then, one by one, dropped to their knees, raised their right had and vowed "I'll promise I will never bait a Catholic again."

"Perfect!" I said, smiling happily. "Now go home, and don't bother me. I've got a Novena to do."

I watched as they walked down the Hill and said to the saints in general, "Aren't they absolutely adorable?"

The answer must have been "yes" because all eight passed.

The Glory Hallelujah

We're gone! The fraternities' parties for the graduating class of 1952 will begin Saturday and go through Sunday. The bath tub gin and juice party, the Giraffe party. The Purple Passion party...all that and more.

So we'll shag and jitterbug to Tommy Dorsey's orchestra at the Saturday night Prom, and we'll bebop and Lindy hop to Benny Goodman at the Saturday afternoon tea dance. The golden years are ahead of us.

Our schedule looks something like this:

Monday, we hang around

Tuesday, we graduate

Wednesday, we start packing

And, within four days, we're gone.

In the meantime, packages from home begin to arrive daily for both of us: underwear, socks, hose, entire outfits for Perk, entire outfits for me, envelopes enclosed each day with cash for shoes, make-up, a beautiful summer jacket for Perk. These from my father. Then one, special fat envelope for Perk.

My Mom and Dad arrive for graduation loaded with a roast turkey, side dishes, dips, potato chips, gin and champagne! And Roses sweetened lime juice for French 75's!

The Perkinsons arrive with little, and a one hundred dollar bill. My attitude is decidedly un-Christian about the matter. He is the first college graduate, ever, in the history of his family; and I want them to be elated and openly proud of him. But that doesn't happen like I'd dreamed.

We just slide on past the situation to the most joyful, zany week I've ever known.

Even the packing is fun! Each night, we put feasts of food on the tables outside. We can't take it with us, so we eat and drink royally, then crash on the blankets spread under the stars.

Even after going to bed, we hear low, murmuring voices now and then, coming form the other groups talking into the early hours stretched out on their blankets.

The leavings and good-byes increase each day. The genuine love and regard among friends is obvious, and tears often show in the eyes of male and female alike.

"Ohhh, I hate leaving," I hear.

"It's gonna seem funny not going to school and seeing you guys every day..." I hear.

"I'm going to miss Copeley Hill," I hear.

"I'm not going to miss it!" I say to myself. "Huhn, what's to miss?

The End

60844547R00074

Made in the USA
Lexington, KY
21 February 2017